I
Can Only Touch You Now

RONALD B. LEVY
Citrus College

Prentice-Hall, Inc., Englewood Cliffs, New Jersey

1 75 $3.95

Library of Congress Cataloging in Publication Data

Levy, Ronald B
    I can only touch you now.

    Bibliography: p.
    1. Conduct of life. I. Title.
BJ1581.2.L48   170'.202   72-8446
ISBN 0-13-448746-X
ISBN 0-13-448738-9 (pbk)

Printed in the United States of America

10 9 8 7 6 5 4 3 2 1

Prentice-Hall International, Inc., *London*
Prentice-Hall of Australia, Pty. Ltd., *Sydney*
Prentice-Hall of Canada, Ltd., *Toronto*
Prentice-Hall of India Private Limited, *New Delhi*
Prentice-Hall of Japan, Inc., *Tokyo*

To my children, Richard, Jim, and Debbie

They touch me now
even though I am very far away

Contents

v

Contents

11

The Encounter: As a Way of Wrestling with God

97

12

The Encounter: As a Way of Teaching

104

13

What Did You Learn in School Today?

117

14

The Reasonableness of Irrationality

125

15

Expectations: Life or Death of Relationships?

132

16

After Now: What?

141

Contents

Preface

The ideas in this book have touched within me for some time.

They came together in a conceptual and very emotional way on a Sunday morning in April 1971 as I was concluding my first honeymoon with my wife, Dolores Ferrell.

They were given a name—a title—later on that same April during a very touchful three-way conversation with Ed Lugenbeel and my wife.

They were fully launched into life in October 1971 when Prentice-Hall contracted with me to finish the book.

This rapid pace did not seem rapid while it was happening. It was only possible, however, because of the continual support and sharp critical advice of my wife. It was she who knew how to phrase a suggestion so that it would touch home constructively and not be taken defensively. It was she who showed me how to apply the ideas about which I was writing. In a very real sense, this book is a collaboration with her. All who benefit from it will owe her a debt of gratitude. And my debt to her can only be paid and repaid by continually touching her—now!

I am again indebted to my typist, Delinda Gloss, who suffered, bled, and almost died in typing her way clearly through the tangle of my hand-written pages.

I am finally indebted to Edward Lugenbeel of Prentice-Hall for his liberal understanding and acceptance of what we are trying to do here.

RONALD LEVY

I think I have
never felt so
completely worthless,
so broken, so apart
in my life!!
Yet this feeling
is mine!
What do I do with it?
How do I relate to it?
It is here with me
Now!

I THINK I HAVE
NEVER FELT SO
VALUABLE AND
TOGETHER IN
MY WHOLE LIFE!
AND THIS FEELING
IS <u>MINE!</u> WHAT
WILL I DO WITH IT?
HOW DO I KEEP
IT? IT IS HERE
WITH ME <u>NOW!</u>

1

Here and Now
As Opposed To
There and Then

The two previous pages each state a condition, a feeling. Each one pervades, permeates, saturates the speaker. It tells "where he is at." If we asked the speaker of the first one to enlarge on his statement, he might say:

"I have been rejected by my lover. I have failed at my job. I can't ever seem to get ahead because *they* don't accept me—give me a chance. It was like this as a child. My mother was never satisfied with what I did. It was never good enough for her. In school, it was the same story—never could seem to do what those teachers wanted. I always missed the boat. I guess I wasn't cut out to be a success. So I might as well get used to being worthless—but I can't. It hurts too bad. Right in my gut! Could it be something I ate? I wonder what makes me feel like this? Maybe if I read some of those new psychology books I might understand why I feel this way. I'm really not sure *what* to do!"

The second speaker is of a different sort. He might expand his statement by saying:

"I have really hit it off well lately. I just got a big promotion at work—and after only a year with the company! My last years in college were a success. And I did pretty well in high school too. But this promotion is really the best yet. Now I can get married and provide for my family. Joan and I have planned for this for a long time. I can put 10 percent down on a house. At my new salary—and with the other raises I am sure to get—I can pay off the mortgage in less than twenty years. We will be secure, and I can provide for Joan and our kids, too, when they come along. What else could I possibly want?"

Both speakers are trying to explain their present situation—to give meaning to it. Each is pervaded by what seems to be an entirely different emotional tone. The first one is negative, pessimistic, discouraged. The second is positive, optimistic, encouraged. They each want to understand where they are. But they are trying to do it by referring to somewhere else—somewhere they aren't. When they try to look at their feelings, they get into explanations. They do not want to look at the Here and Now. They both would rather look at the There and Then.

The first speaker is immersed in his past experiences—what has been. He looks to his past as a kind of explanation of his plight in the present. Of course he can't change the past—or so he believes. So he uses the past to excuse his present. If he can do this, then it is clear that the present is not his fault. No one can blame him! Yet we get the feeling that he does feel a bit resentful, if not guilty, about his present situation. And he does not see any way out of his morass of failure and. pain. We can't really believe that reading psychology books will do any more than help him confirm how worthless he is—in psychological terms. He may go on playing the "poor me" game forever.

The second speaker is immersed in his future. He has almost forgotten the past—except as it leads to his successful present and his even more-to-be-successful future. He is a man of future triumphs, future experiences—not only for himself, but for his family-to-be also. He does not have them now. Yet they are already successfully on hand and secure—in his mind. His success is so pure and undiluted that one might mistake his final question for a purely rhetorical one. On second reading, it may be clearer that this question, "What

2

else could I possibly want?" could be the clue to his life style. He may really not know what to want *now*, since his meanings are mostly drawn from, and related to, the future. The meanings of his present life are therefore just as vacant as those of the first speaker whose meanings are largely drawn from the past. Yet most of us—particularly those who feel we are caught in the painful past—would gladly change places with this second speaker. However, he escapes from his Now by his ladder to future successes—never really appreciating, in the present, this family which he planned for so clearly.

These two speakers are examples of how one can get caught in the There and Then. The first speaker's There and Then is the past. The second speaker's is the future. But each speaker is avoiding the Here and Now. His attention is continually turned away from what *is* going on to what *has been* or *will be* going on. Number One does mention a feeling—a pain in his gut. But he does not stay with it, and he escapes from his present awareness of it by trying to explain it. Number Two never mentions a feeling at all, except in his original statement. In his expanded statement, he is bathed in the rosy glow of the future which may become purple or blue if he does not regularly come back to touch the Now.

All of us must spend some time in the There and Then. We must remember, or recommit the errors of the past. We must plan, or run headlong into impending walls and barricades. However this is not where we live. And in order to live, we must return regularly to the Delphic oasis of the Here and Now to be refreshed and reborn. At this oasis we may learn many ways to be warmed and revitalized; to be strengthened and loved; to come together and withdraw. Among other things, we may learn that touch is the most personal of all experiences. It sounds through all the masks which culture and civilization have made to hide and separate us. We may learn that the colors of touch are many and varied—that the harmonic and dissonant weaving of the patterns of touch are amazing and confusing. But no matter how I touch or am touched, and no matter what the design and form of the patterns of touch, I will find that I am only touched now, and I can only touch you now. If you doubt this, ask yourself if you are ever kissed—or slapped—*then*?

This means that touch is the gateway to the experience of the Now—

and through this gateway pass those on the road to the land of increasing awareness—both of self and others.

In more prosaic terms, one might translate this by saying, "don't fuck up your Now with plans for who you will fuck, or did fuck, then. For even Solomon with all his concubines was not as well supplied as you, who are attuned to the richness of your Now!"

And now, what are YOU aware of? What are YOU feeling after such an introduction? Will you write down here—at the bottom of this page—just how you feel now? Or will you escape by leaving it blank or by writing a long list of rationalized explanations from your head and by so doing turn yourself off?

2

Awareness

The Ground of the Now

"I am tingling all over. I feel waves of emotion surging over and through me."

"I am cold and deadened. My hands and feet are lifeless and my head and neck are rigid and numb."

"I am resentfuly, angry. My head throbs. And yet my face is a veneered mask which separates me from all others."

"I tremble with fear. My mouth is dry and my throat is strained and tense. I can hardly speak."

All of these statements speak awareness. They tell of feelings going on now in the bodies of several people—waves of emotion, coldness and numbness, throbbing, trembling, tenseness. In each case the feeling is an event—something which is happening—and the person is focusing his attentiveness on what is happening. He is aware. And this awareness puts him in the Now. (He is never aware *then*.) It is as though there is a contact taking place *in* his body. Things are coming together—are touching—and it is this touching *and* the attentiveness to it which is the awareness. There must be a touch—a contact—to be attentive to. And I must be attentive to this touch as well if I am to be aware.

For example, we are sitting together having dinner at our favorite restaurant. I touch your leg. This is an event—a bodily event. There is something happening. I have touched you. But you may not be aware of my touch. You may be engrossed and attentive to your food—or to the look on the face of the man at the next table. You may not be attentive to my touch at all. You will only be *aware* of my touch if you turn your attentiveness to your leg and feel the touch of my hand there. Then you will be aware of my touch. If you choose to turn off your attentiveness to your leg, then my hand may as well not be there. For you are not aware of it at all, and the point of my touching you is lost. I can touch you now, but my touch needs your attentiveness to it to complete it in your awareness.

But isn't touch a thing of hands, of skin, of the outside of me? It is easy to see how I can be aware of a touch on my arm or leg, or a slap on my cheek. These are skin contacts. They are external bodily events. But how can I be touched *in* my body? In the first place can an external agent touch *inside* me? Can a call or message touch me—really—inside? Can what is outside produce waves, throbbing tenseness, be trembling *inside* me? And in the second place, what about those purely internal feelings which seem to arise for no external reason at all—can those be considered touches? Is there any way in which a headache or muscle cramp could be considered a touch? Do they have anything in common with a slap or a kiss? Let us consider first the kind of internal bodily events which seem to have an external agent.

"I am touched by the sob in his voice."
"I am touched by the pitiful face of the hungry child."
"I am thrilled by the letter I received from my lover."
"His remark cuts deep into my heart—touches my soul."

These are internal touches—not just of the skin or hands. They certainly speak awareness too! They are examples of awareness which *seem* to have an outside agent. And these agents seem to touch inside and arouse the attentiveness of the speakers.

"I have a splitting headache—couldn't sleep all night!"
"My stomach is bloated and painful. My digestion is bad."

"My leg muscles are cramped. I can't seem to relax them."
"I feel tired and exhausted. I ache all over!"

These are internal feelings too. They do not seem to have an external agent. I certainly am aware of these feelings. But are they in any sense touches?

There are, then, three kinds of bodily events to which I can be attentive and by doing so become aware of them. First, the strictly external events—the skin-to-skin contact, the kiss, the kick, the caress. Second, the external events where the agent *seems* to touch inside—the look of love, the song of the meadowlark, the smell of pine wood burning. Third, the strictly internal events where the touch or contact is wholly within—the heart beat, the headache, the pain of fatigue. There is a contact—a coming together—a touch in each case. Even in the headache or fatigue there is a muscular and neural movement, a bodily tension and contraction, to which one gives his attentiveness in order to be aware. Were there no bodily change at all in muscle, in nervous system, in body chemistry, or in energy level, there would be no event to be attentive to and hence no awareness. Were there an anesthesia in that part of the body where the touch occurred—in the arm, face, muscle, nerve or organ—there would also be no awareness. Touch and attentivness are both necessary for awareness in all of these examples.

Ok, so now we know what awareness is and the various varieties of awareness. We also know what it takes to be aware. But what does awareness do for me? What is the point of being aware? Would I not be better off if I were less aware? Sometimes I feel painfully aware of too much—or so it seems!

I have just arrived in a strange town. I check into my motel room. I am alone. I feel painfully alone. I think of all the interesting companions I would like to have with me now. This makes my awareness of my loneliness even more intense—so intense that I cannot stand it. I go to the nearest bar. There I am bound to find others—or at least another—who is also lonely. There, at least, we can talk, relate, be friendly. Perhaps I can even find someone to "fill up" my loneliness on a longer term basis. A few drinks to anesthetize my loneliness will help the process. Then I am ready to relate more effectively to another. Is it

7

not better in such a situation to reduce the *pain* of my intense awareness?

There is no necessary answer to this question. It depends on whether I want to be able to control—to be responsible for my actions, feelings, and emotions—or not. For if control of my self is what I want, then awareness is not just desirable, it is necessary. Without awareness, no control. With awareness, control is not guaranteed, but it becomes increasingly possible as the awareness grows. If I go to the bar and anesthetize my loneliness, I will lose some of my inhibitions and perhaps be able to talk to a stranger more easily. But what I do not realize is that I will also anesthetize my ability to deal with my underlying fears and insecurities as well. These are the real cause of my loneliness. Therefore my talk will probably be less controlled and less nourishing to whomever I may find in the bar. Add to this that my bar companion is probably "empty" too and poorly qualified to fill me up, and I have the makings of a rather unfortunate evening. Were I willing to stay with the pain of my loneliness, I might become even more intensely aware—more fully aware in a together and integrated sense—and thus be able to move toward the first steps in controlling my loneliness. Let us now look a bit further into the various types of bodily events described above and the kinds of awareness associated with them.

Consider the first kind of awareness—the awareness of touch from an external source, the skin or body contact awareness. I feel a touch on my hand. I am aware of it. Since I am aware of the touch, I can repond to it. I can move my arm away. I can reach out further toward whatever is touching. I can remain motionless and aware and enjoy, or suffer with, this touch. Or I can turn off my attention and become unaware of the touch and act as though it didn't exist. This I would probably do only if the touch seemed to produce highly ambivalent feelings in me. In this case, since I would be no longer aware, I would no longer have control. Nor could I be responsible. This might be the case with my dinner companion whom I described above. My hand on her leg may leave her confused as to my intentions. She may also be confused as to what she would like my intentions to be. This ambivalence leaves her in a quandary as to how to respond. So she "anesthetizes" her leg by turning her attentiveness from it and does not "know" my hand is there. Then she need not decide how to respond. She is no longer aware. She has relieved herself of responsibility.

But she *can* control her behavior with respect to the touch. She has a choice about what she will do. She *can* choose how she will move or not move. She *can* choose how to direct or turn off her attentiveness. And since she can do all these things, she can be responsible for her behavior.

Now there is another aspect of this situation besides mere bodily movements. There is the way I feel about the touch—whether I enjoy it or whether I suffer with it. Can I control and be responsible for this too?

Suppose I am with a close companion of the opposite sex—my wife, or my lover. We become separated from each other in a crowd as we leave a large auditorium. The light is dim, and I cannot see too well. I become upset at not being able to find her. In my search for her, a hand touches me, and I think it is hers. I am at first relieved. But as I turn toward the hand, I find it is someone else's. My relief changes to some other emotion—probably confusion. If it is a man whose hand I feel, I am likely to be even more confused.

What caused these emotions? Why did I become upset? Or better, *how* did I become upset? How did I become relieved? How did my feelings change—or become confused? Am I responsible for these feelings at all? If so, to what extent?

It seems clear that I became upset when I became aware of the absence of my companion. If I were not aware of her absence, I certainly would not be upset about it. *Her* absence did not cause the upset. It was *my* awareness of her absence which caused it. And my awareness—my attentiveness to her, or to any other element in my life—is an act of my choosing. I can develop and be more and more attentive to whatever I choose. (Ways of developing greater attentiveness will be discussed in a subsequent chapter.) Therefore, in one sense I am responsible for being upset in so far as my attentiveness is a matter of my own choosing.

But this is not all of it. Certainly I must be aware of her absence to be upset by it. But how is it that I am upset and not something else? Is it necessary that such an absence produce an upsetting feel-

9

ing? Obviously, this is not the case as many people are not upset by the absence of a companion, and others may even be relieved. On occasion I am relieved by someone's absence. Do I, then, upset myself? Or is the upset produced by something over which I have no control?

Here one has a choice to make as to how he sees himself and others. Are we self-directing beings who can potentially control our own behavior with increasing effectiveness if we want to do so? Or are we pawns in a game of chance, moved about by powers over which we have little or no influence? If it is the latter, then we must seek to propitiate the Gods of Chance. Or become active in the manifold efforts, now currently in vogue, to change the nature of the society and culture which seem to inhibit us. Without getting into the debate as to the possibility of either of these alternatives, let us say that human beings are at least potentially self-directing and therefore can be responsible and learn to control their behavior—even to the feelings and emotions they have. We will go on, in the next chapter, to see how I may, in fact, upset myself. For if I understand this, I then have at my disposal the means for controlling my upset. But let us turn now to the other kinds of feelings and awareness which were mentioned earlier. How about the relief at the touch of a hand, and the sub-sequent confusion at my recognition that it is the hand of a stranger?

Of course my relief is part of my scenario. I picture the hand as hers. She has come back. I am again at least potentially in con-trol. Even more so, perhaps, since she did "obediently" return to me after the absence. I may unload a bit of my momentary upset on her. But after all she is here now. My relief is great because so was my upset. Had I chosen merely to interpret her absence as a necessary trip to the restroom or a stop at a drinking fountain, then her return would have been much less of a relief. But this scenario would not have allowed me to discipline her as much. And so my need to behave in this way would have been frustrated. It is almost as though I wanted her to "misbehave" so I could test my controlling power. When one insists that behavior—ours or another's—takes place according to a precisely set series of expectations, we whip up our adrenals to a froth repeatedly. Life usually refuses to comply with such insistent demands—particularly human life. And this refusal, which we really produce by our demands, upsets us. When we drop our demand that others perform up to our expectations, life is calmer, less tense, but more exciting, since newness is free to enter and delicious surprises are on every hand. We feel relieved. And if we will accept and be attentive to such feelings, it it possible for us to control. And we can control relief as well. For relief, in this case, means I have regained control— either by relaxing my demands on another or on myself. The simple return of my companion is likely, at best, to produce only a temporary relief. "How glad I am that you are here! Please don't ever do that again!"If she is at all red blooded, she certainly will do it again. And if I keep up my insistent demands, my control can at best be very short lived.

The confusion at the touch of a stranger is another matter. If I am uptight—unaware—I am usually a person whose repertory of touch is rather narrow. I am probably not often touched. And when I am it is by relatively few persons. A touch by a female companion who is close to me is, at most, a relief, an assurance that she is there under control. A touch by a stranger is confusing since the possible scenario in which to place it is vague. If I am uptight, I wonder *why* am I being touched by this stranger—particularly if he is a man. "What do you want from me?" I think. And it shows on my face. I do not pay much attention to *how* I am touched. Therefore my awareness of the touch, and the context in which it occurs, is marginal and piecemeal. I am confused because I do not listen or pay attention to the various overtones of the touch. Is it a touch of influence, of gentleness, of aggression, or of invitation? Does he want to push me out of his way so he can leave in a hurry? Does he sense my confusion and upset and is he seeking to calm me? Is he resentful towards me for some unconscious aggressive act of mine? Or is he inviting me to relate to him in some unknown—and, to me, frightening—way?

Since I am poorly schooled in touching and being touched, I do not know. And since I cannot face (be attentive to) myself, and cannot control myself, I would usually seek to control this other person, at least as far as his behavior relates to me. This I cannot easily do since I am not adequately aware of him or me. I will tend to pull away from him and resent his touch for fear of being dominated or losing whatever control I imagine I have over myself. But I hesitate because I do not

11

know, and I do not want to be abrupt in this public gathering. Hence I am confused. I freeze. And my feelings show only in the tenseness of my face.

Again, all this would be of no concern were I adequately aware. Then I would be tuned in to the message of the touch. Then I would realize that I create my response to it. Then I could accept the touch as another part of my experience and let it lead me where it may without my need to dominate or be dominated by it. This might lead me to a new and enriching friendship—through the magic of accepting a touch.

All that has been said so far is about external touch and awareness— the skin contact touch. What about the various types of awareness to internal touches—the external agent that touches inside, and the purely internal touch of awareness? Am I also responsible for these too?

Yes, of course I am—at least as far as my awareness is based on my attentiveness. We have seen that my attentiveness is a conscious act on my part. I can be attentive if I want to learn to be. But we must remember that there are two aspects of this type of external-internal touching. There is the awareness of the external agent. And there is the awareness of internal touch. There is the awareness of the song, the look, the smell. And there is the awareness of the internal bodily tingle, tenseness, or revulsion associated with them. I can certainly choose, by focusing my attentiveness, to be aware of either or both of these aspects of the touching. In this sense I am certainly responsible for my awareness of these events.

But, again, we come to the qualitative aspects of these bodily events and touches—the kinds of feelings associated with them. The song may sadden me or make me happy. The look may excite me or terrify me. The smell may disgust me or attract me. Am I responsible for these differences? If so, how? Is there really an external *agent*— someone or something that is outside of me that acts on me? Or is it merely the external situations—those things around me—to which I react?

This is a bit harder to explain than the purely external awareness of a touch and my response to it. How am I saddened by a song or frightened by a look? Can I with any validity say, "I sadden myself

when I hear Joan Baez sing *What Have They Done To The Rain?"*
Can I say, "I frighten myself when I see the look of distress on my
lover's face?" If so, how do I sadden myself? How do I frighten
myself?

Certainly the external agent is not saddening or frightening in itself. Not everyone is saddened by the same song or frightened by the
same look. Nor am I always saddened or frightened by any particular
song or look, although sadness may quite regularly tend to be
associated with some special song, or fear with some particular person's
look. If this is so, then it would seem that *I* am the agent of sadness or
fear. *I* produce it.

But what exactly do I do to sadden myself or frighten myself? Again
I believe it is the scenario I create in my mind and the attentiveness I
have to my bodily processes. If I am saddened by the song, it is because
I choose to create a scenario related to the song where I am playing a
sad or pitiful role. I am a little boy left alone. I am a parent bereft of a
child. I am a lover who has been spurned. I play this sad role and in so
doing release a pool of sadness which I have previously kept
repressed. I also make myself sad by being attentive to the feelings in
my eyes, to my breathing, and to my voice and throat. If I turned all of
these things off and if I did not choose the sad scenario, I would not
make myself sad.

I make myself frightened by choosing a fearful scenario. I see myself
being attacked, punished, threatened, by the person who looks
"menacingly" at me. In this scenario I release the accumulated fear
which I have kept hidden, and I help it along by being attentive to my
pulse, my breathing, and the wide-open feeling of my eyes, the sensations in my skin and sweat glands. If I were not attentive to these
signs of fear and did not choose the fearful scenario, I would not be
frightened.

"But," you will say, "My fear—or sadness—is involuntary. I do not
choose any of these things." Yes, it seems that way to one who is not
together—to one who has many residual pools of emotional energy
stored in his body. If I want to control my sadness, or fear, the
procedure is clear. It is quite similar to what was mentioned before. I
must develop a heightened awareness to bodily sensations and to the
way these develop in relation to mental images and fan-

13

tasies. Furthermore, control cannot be developed in the face of large amounts of stored emotional energy. So if I want to master and be able to express my emotions—of fear or sadness, for example—when I want to do so, I first need to be aware of, and release regularly, my accumulations of emotional energy and tension. I need to realize that I can choose whatever scenario I want to play in response to external stimuli, and I need to be attentive to the bodily mechanisms which are the signs of a particular emotion. If I want to be sad, I pay attention to my throat and breathing (my sobbing mechanism), and also to my eyes (my crying mechanism). If my reservoir of sadness and tension is too full, I may cry when I want to laugh or be angry. If I am not attentive to the scenario I choose or to my bodily signs of emotion, I may not be able to cry at all when I am sad. But through the development of heightened and deepened awareness, emotions can be expressed in ways that make life more meaningful and rewarding. In other words I can be responsible for their mode and depth of expression. There is no external agent. The agent who produces the emotion is me!

Now to the purely internal bodily events—the heartbeat, the headache, the pain of fatigue. Is there any touch here? Can I control or be responsible for the feelings or emotions associated with them?

Yes, there certainly is a kind of touch, though not of the skin. Certainly my blood and heart chambers and blood vessels touch and are touched. Furthermore, I can become increasingly aware of my pulse. And with practice, using meters to show the change in blood pressure and pulse rate, I can learn to be more attentive to my pulse and so control it. If this is so, can I not make my pulse beat faster and so increase and reinforce the emotional expression of fear? Can I not increase the expression of fatigue by reducing my pulse rate? And can I not counteract these feelings by doing the reverse?

But do I, or can I, give myself a headache? Is there any touch there? Yes, there is a constriction in head and neck muscles and blood vessels which is an important factor in producing a headache. This constriction is a touching of tissue against tissue. It is usually produced in response to a need to resist some form of external domination. In other words, when I am pushed around by some external agent and am not free to respond and express my resistance or resentment externally, I do so internally in my neck and head and so produce a headache. I

14

become "stiff-necked." This usually affects my blood circulation and neural energy flow as well.

Am I responsible for this feeling? Can I master it? Yes, if I turn my attentiveness to the pain and follow its movement and pulse, it may change, move, or diminish. I may feel it move from my head and neck to my shoulders and back, to my jaws, or to my hands and arms. As this happens, I may pick up the idea that I am holding back the expression of resentment, probably toward someone who is near and dear to me. It may be my lover whom I resent. She dominates me in such a sweet gentle way as she "asks" for my attention. I resent her soft control, her requests which seem to say, "You may do as you wish, darling, but anyone who really loved me would want to always be with me." Or it may be a parent whom I resent—my mother who is continually playing on my guilt to get me to do things her way. "Of course you may dress as you want to, my son. And I am so proud of you when you wear your hair in that short, dignified way which your father and I always liked so much. But, of course, we want you to know that your life is your own."

I would not dare to express my resentment to my lover. She would cut off my water. She wouldn't love me any more. And my mother is so tender and fragile. She would fall apart if I told her how I feel. She couldn't take it. So I repress my resentment, and I forget that it is even there, and it surfaces in my head and neck.

When I do go with my pain and let it "talk" to me, I am presented with a new course of action other than suffering, escape, or drugs. With this awareness, I gain the power to be responsible. I can keep this headache or I can lose it. The course is open to me. All I need to do is to release my resentment in some nonpunitive way, if I want to lose it. And the change is likely to take place immediately. (For more on this see chapters 5 and 6.) On the other hand, if I take pills, or try to escape the pain in other ways, the ache is likely to continue to stay, or at best leave only temporarily.

Is this true of all headaches? Perhaps not. Some headaches may come from acidity in the body due to poor diet or excessive eating or drinking. But these excesses are, of course, responses to some form of emotional need—perhaps the need to escape the feeling of rejection or failure. If I am aware of my body, its feelings, its processes, and its needs, I can choose to overeat or drink, or choose not to do so. If am not adequately aware of my body, I can not be responsible. I will overeat or drink involuntarily in response to emotional conditions, or I will hold in my resentment, not realizing that to do so produces my headache by means of the muscular tensions in head and neck.

We have now covered the three types of awareness—the external, the external-internal, and the strictly internal. All involve a bodily event— a kind of touch or change in the body. All are associated with feelings. All can be developed by learning to be attentive to the various parts and processes of the body. All are a necessary part of developing responsible and controlled behavior—not only of gross bodily movements but of emotions and fine bodily movements as well. This is what awareness can do for anyone. And, furthermore, awareness is always *now*, so in addition increased awareness means living life more fully. In the next chapter, we return to the matter of upsetting my self and how I do it. In a later chapter we will explore how to develop awareness through the magic of touch.

3

How Do I Upset Myself?

There are many ways by which I upset myself. In the example of chapter 2, where I am suddenly aware that my companion is missing, it might go somewhat like this. Prior to her absence, I am secure and warm in the association with her. Perhaps I have enjoyed a play or concert with her and am looking forward now to sharing her company more fully in many ways later on. Suddenly she is gone. I turn to look for her. She is nowhere in sight. The foyer is too dimly lit to see very far or clearly. My mind races ahead attempting to imagine where she might be, how she might have disappeared. All sorts of tragedies present themselves although they are, of course, the creations of my own mind. She may have been lured away by something else, she may be dazed and lost in the crowd. She may desire to be free of my company and may wish to avoid the rest of the evening which I anticipate so much. As my mind generates these alternate scenarios, I settle on one, perhaps the last. I elaborate on it, and as I do I become more and more tense and at a loss. In essence I am suffering from a lack of control. I would like to influence her presence—her absence. I do not want her to leave or yield to some other lure. I do not want her to be dazed. I do not want her to avoid me or my plans. I want to dominate her behavior, and this I cannot do if she is absent—even though I may not control her too well when she is present. Her absence absolutely takes away my influence on her, and in so doing I lose control of myself. I choose and generate my own upsetting, and I produce my loss of control by the mental fantasies which I, in fact, create.

It is pointless to debate or seek to understand *why* I create these fantasies instead of others. If I am *aware* that I create them and I could just as well create others, I have a way out of my upset. What I need, then, is a greater awareness of myself and my behavior. Besides the awareness that I create my fantasies, I need to be attentive to the bodily sensations I have as I experience the absence of my companion. I need to be attentive to my rising feeling of being upset as I create my fantasies. I need to be able to follow all of these events in my body. As I do this, I gain a fuller awareness of myself. I gain a mastery of myself and my feelings and fantasies. And I lose the need to dominate some other person. I am free of the need to control another, and I have control of myself.

When I am uptight and not together, it is painful to be attentive to myself. I have learned, unfortunately, to avoid pain. Therefore the slightest attention to my split-up, divided self drives me to something or someone else to be attentive to. It may be training a dog or horse. It may be building exact models of airplanes or railroad trains. Or it may be controlling someone else—a wife, a lover, a child, or a friend. I am OK as long as I can successfully carry out the details of control in these activities. I am symbolically putting myself together—controlling myself in this other activity. But when I am separated from this activity or when the object of my control disappears, I am thrown back again on my own devices. It is painful to be attentive to myself so I cannot do that. I have failed in my efforts to symbolically control. So I seek to find a new object of control. Or I enter into the act of destroying that which I cannot control—including myself. If I cannot control, constructively, I can at least control destructively.

I can enter into the act of self-destruction through drugs, liquor, or any other toxic means, and I can attempt to lure the object of my control—if it is to be a person—into my destructive vortex. In this way I have negatively controlled my growth and development. I have in-

18

sured that I can *not* be successful. And how much better if I can also have company in this macabre celebration! We can meet night after night and cooperatively *prove* that we can not be successful, while we are gradually destroying that which could make us successful—our bodily awareness.

Another way in which I might upset myself could be centered around my need to release a pool of accumulated hostility. My companion may have been quite attentive to me, but I may have experienced a series of frustrations in other dimensions of my life. I may be in line for a promotion in my work which I feel was unjustly given to another instead of me. An unexpected bill may have arrived which I am ill-prepared to pay. My mother may be demanding my attention and I am resentful—but guilty—about this. The sudden absence of my companion may be the straw that breaks the camel's back. But more than this, her absence gives me an excuse—a real excuse, I think—to be upset, even though I am not consciously aware of this. So I look and wait for her. I dream up the most exaggerated duplicity on her part. She has met some old lover and has slipped away with him. And I know just who he is—that glib swinger she talked to so much at the party last Saturday. Didn't he say he was going to this play too? I begin to seethe. And when I finally see her ahead of me talking to a man, I am at the exploding point. It makes no difference if it is her brother, her next-door neighbor, or a complete stranger in the city asking directions to a nearby night club. My feeling is the same. And I use this event—her "unexcused" absence—to whip up my latent hostility and thereby unload it at my innocent companion's expense. Needless to say this is likely to destroy any pleasure which lay in store for me the rest of the evening.

A third way of upsetting myself is by setting the kind of scene in which my upset is likely to occur. There may be many such scenes. They depend on my style of life. It may be that I am prone to get uptight and upset when I am tired and fatigued. If so, a great way to upset myself would be to wait to tackle a knotty problem or enter into a crucial discussion until I am fatigued. Or it may be that it is my partner—wife, lover, or other close associate—who is particularly affected when fatigue develops. If I press ahead in a serious discussion when my partner is on the verge of fatigue, then it is fairly certain that we both will be upset. The more compulsively I press the discussion, the greater the fatigue. And the greater the fatigue, the less our ability to deal with each other calmly and rationally. Hence the upset grows beyond all bounds, and we are mutually trapped in an uproar. All I need to know is that fatigue in myself or my partner is extremely disorganizing and is a sure formula for producing an upsetting situation.

But this may be only one of many potentially upset-producing situations. I may be upset-prone on the first of the month when all the bills come due. I may feel that I cannot handle my financial problems and this gets me down. I feel that I should be able to do this. Or I may be upset-prone at the time of menstruation. I feel I cannot handle my bodily well-being and this "cramps" my style. It may be—strange to say—that I get upset at vacation time when plans for trips and travel must be made. I cannot make detailed decisions of a nonroutine nature easily. And this kills the spontaneity of my vacation. The specific cause or situation is irrelevant. The important point is that I *know* that at certain times and under certain conditions upset is likely to occur—usually due to a feeling that neither my partner or I are coping too well with life. If I know this, then I can easily set the stage for a grand upset by pressing compulsively to discuss and deal with matters of great difficulty—heavy personal problems—at such times. Since these problems usually require great calmness, reason, energy, understanding, and open-mindedness to deal with them effectively, if I insist on discussing them when my partner or I are under a strain or in a delicate emotional balance, it will usually guarantee that I will be overloaded, emotionally incapacitated, and poorly prepared to deal with the problems, and therefore will be badly upset.

"But," you say, "I do not *plan* to be upset *ever*! And neither does my wife (although sometimes I wonder). I try to avoid major emotional upsets like the curse! They are nerve-racking, debilitating, exhausting. They leave me wrung out for days!"

Well, I hear what you say. But if this is true, you would avoid at all costs the potentially upset-producing situations and times. Nothing— no problem—*has* to be discussed at a bad or upsetting time. It could wait if *you* could wait. But you want to produce upset. You want to upset yourself. So you choose a time which can't lose. It becomes a self-fulfilling prophesy. You know it will happen. So to prove you are right, you choose the perfect time.

You know that your lover is unreasonable about money, so you prove it. You insist on discussing it when she is exhausted. You know it costs too much to go to Europe, and you could never work out the details, so you propose that you and your wife discuss this matter during the first days of her menstrual period. This proves that it can't be done. Your prophesy comes true. You know that you have lost your creative ability as a painter or writer, so you prove it by trying to sandwich in your creativity after an exhausting day at your office or the day after a heavy drinking bout. You know that you are overweight and unattractive. So you prove it by standing in front of the mirror and looking at yourself on the first of the month after all the bills have come in and you know you can pay only half of them and all the world looks black! You know you are losing your sexual potency. So you prove it by trying to make love after six martinis, a bottle of wine, and two afterdinner drinks. And you are right. You do strike out! In each case, you make the prophesy and you see to it that it is fulfilled. And now you are upset about the result. But not completely. Because inside you have *proven* you are right!

Again I turn to the age old question, "Why do I do this to myself? Why do I give myself and those close to me such pain and discomfort?" If I get into this kind of analysis, I must leave my body, leave the here and now, and go into the past of there and then, of child rearing, of schooling, of adolescent peer groups, etc. And I may never—if I ever do find the "why"—know what to do about it *now*. Therefore you or I, if we would live a fuller, less upsetting life, must focus on how—and how *right now*—do I upset myself. This may give an answer. The "why" can only confuse me with guilt and regret.

So now we see how I can upset myself. What can I do about it? Well, I can choose to be upset, if this suits my life style. I may be typically upset and feel that this is a comfortable way of life for me since I am used to it. Should I want to lose my condition of being upset, I would need to become more attentive to what is going on around me, and this I can only do if I become more aware of what is going on within me. My instrument for being aware is my body and all its accompanying organs of sensory awareness. Whenever I turn off my body, I become less aware. When I become less aware, I am less together—both in myself and with my surrounding world. This split—this divided feeling—makes it more difficult for me to control myself, and my surroundings. To heal this split, I need to be more attentive to my internal feelings—my pain and discomfort as well as my pleasures. As I do this I will be able to see how I upset myself. I will see the tragic scenarios I choose in order to do this mentally. And I will be able to trace the feelings which flow and generate in my body. As I allow these feelings to flow freely, they will become a real part of me. I will accept them, and as a real part of me they will be within my control since I am aware of them and how *they* operate? No, not really—I am aware of how *I* operate!! If I choose not to suffer the pain—to turn it off by drugs or medicine, food, sleep or sex, or the sentimentality of a friend who spreads unguent on my wounds—then I will become less and less aware, less and less in control, and more and more upset and split. In any case it is my choice. I can be responsible for my feelings if I choose to do so. I can be what I want to be by just being what I am and not worrying about whether I can or not.

4

Plateaus, Peaks, and Valleys of Feeling

"I am forty years old. I have four children aged six to twelve. My husband divorced me for a younger woman. I gave him the best years of my life—and my body. I guess my best was not good enough. Now he is happy—or so he says. He gives me enough to give my children the necessities—the necessities for *them*. But who really wants *me*? I have no satisfying adult relationships with men. I run from one to another. They never seem to want me permanently, deeply. Who would want a forty-year-old woman with four children? I tell my troubles to my girl friends. But they often seem too busy for me too. When my husband visits the children, they run to him with stars in their eyes. I feel empty, directionless, and alone. Lately I am drinking very heavily."

"I am eighteen years old and a freshman in college. I want very much to be an architect. I have a flair for design—or used to have. I designed all the sets for our high school senior play. I am healthy—too healthy. I could pass my physical in great style for induction into the Armed Forces. I have a very low draft number. I am sure to be called soon. I have a girl friend to whom I am very close. We have a beautiful relationship. We want to get married.

But what can I do? I hate war and killing. I don't want to die. But my parents are always after me to be loyal and enlist. I would refuse induction, but that would mean jail. I could split to Canada, but that would mean giving up my country. I could plead or fake homosexuality. But that would violate my innermost feelings—not to mention my family and my girl. I have a great deal I want to do in life, but things are *so* mixed up, confused! I just go on from day to day hoping it will somehow work out— hoping that this mess is all a bad dream and I will wake up. But it just gets more confusing. Why does life have to be such a mess? Lately I find myself looking for ways of escaping. And I have found many escapes which work pretty well too!''

"I am thirty, moderately attractive, and intelligent. But what good does it do me? Of course I don't advertise my attributes. In the company of men, I am never overly aggressive. I must be careful not to shatter their delicate egos. I let them talk unless they are just too stupid and boring. I am a teacher in high school. And I do a good job of stimulating my students to do creative writing—that is, all of them who have any innate ability. Those others no one could help. And I am getting fed up with them. My principal is afraid of me. He has no balls at all, and every time I try a new technique in my classes—which he hears about from a parent—he attempts to hold me back, get me to modify it, or do something else. He is really afraid of his shadow, and he lets those shitty parents push him around like a chip in a wind storm. But schools are like that, and public education is really on the skids. How can you expect stupid yokels on a board of education who have little or no education to tell us what to do? They have only their prejudices and ignorance to guide them.

"This is all most depressing and discouraging to me. I intended to make a career of teaching, but no more! Too much ignorance and duplicity in the high places. What will I do? I don't know— that's what's so depressing. I have to work. I couldn't stand to be married to any man for long. The three I tried were just too in-secure to appreciate me. Business? Merchandising? Selling? Too boring and dull. Too many grasping, money-hungry people. Art? Writing? Music? You've got to be kidding! I don't want to starve, and besides no one appreciates real creative ability anyway. I feel very much alone, and in fact I live mostly alone. And I *don't like it*! But what am I do? There seems to be no one to whom I can relate in a forthright, honest way. They are all too ignorant, frightened, or dishonest!"

These three people are all in their own kind of valley of feeling. They are in the depths. Their depression is one thing they have in common. However they differ in what they see as the cause of their depression. In one it is herself. In another it is circumstances, life. In the third it is people, other people.

If we look more carefully, there is another possible common element in all three. They are all *out of touch* with reality. "But," you will say, "do they not describe reality as they see it?" Yes of course they do. But a reality which appears to be pervaded continuously with only one quality must be, to that extent, a distorted reality. Reality, objective reality, does not have qualities at all. We project our feelings on it—on the external objective world. Those qualities which we perceive arise from our contact with reality. If we are healthy and together in our bodies, we experience an ever-changing cyclic variation of feelings. And our contacts with reality will be correspondingly various. If I am not together in my body, I am out of touch with my body, and correspondingly I am out of touch with reality too. I am touching only partially—in a distorted fashion—and hence I am out of touch. What I do touch is real enough, but I mistake what I touch for *all*! So when I perceive only one universally pervading quality in reality, I am seeing a distorted reality due to my being out of touch.

So the three whose statements we read above are out of touch with reality. Each one is in the depths of his valley of feeling because he is apart, split, not together. He is split from himself, from his body. And he is split from his real world as well. The split from the body is the basic split. And from it arises the split from the world, from life, from other people. The problem for such split, out of touch persons is that they seek to solve the split on the outside while being blind to the split on the inside. It is as though I am looking for the person who is tracking mud on my carpet when the mud is on my own shoes. In order to remove the distortion, I must heal the split in myself—clean my own shoes. Then I can see clearly and directly what I am faced with outside.

So valleys of feeling arise when we are split. What then produces a peak of feeling? Let us listen to the description of several types of peak experiences in the words of those who experienced them. The first one says:

"As I listened to the music, it transported me to another world. I was soaring high over the mountains, over forests and rivers. I could see the flowing of rushing water and smell the fresh greenness of the trees. As the music progressed, I would rise and fall in my flight—sometimes dropping abruptly and feeling as though my stomach were charged with electricity. Sometimes there was a precipitous climb to new heights followed by a gradual soaring on wings high above the earth, and a feeling of dizziness in my head. I was supremely confident as I glided, dived, and climbed. My head might get dizzy and light, or my stomach vibrate, but it was my dizziness and my vibration and I thrilled with it! When the music stopped, I was tingling all over as though I were a new person fused together and vibrating with my own particular music—and at one with the world!"

The second one says:

"As we moved toward the band, my body had already picked up the beat and was resonating with the music. We edged ourselves on to the floor and started moving and vibrating with the music. I felt fluid and ready for the challenge as I saw her pick up the rhythm and go it one better in her own variation. I did my own thing now—responding now to the music and now to her movements. As the volume and tempo rose, I felt a pulsating surge go through my body. Now it was in my chest, now my gut and groin, now my legs, now all over me. I flowed like a fountain of rhythmic motion. I was of one piece in a powerful, ecstatic way. Whatever came from the music or her, I could match and blend with—or extend even further if need be. There was no sense of fatigue, and when the music ended I felt free and exhilarated!"

The third one says:

"I sat down to write as though there were no other person, no other place, no other thoughts but mine. The words flowed from my pen, and the paper seemed to draw them out. They did not come by my power, but flowed through me as though they came from another source. I watched them come, and directed them whenever I could. Often they did not seem to fit as I wanted them to. And when I tried to direct them, they refused. At times this turned them off entirely. But I caught the flow again and gave it its head. Now the surge was even greater, the current stronger, and the spray higher. I was riding it with full confidence though I did not know its direction. I was carried along by the torrent, and when it came to a conclusion, it was not an end. The current rode on. But I had been carried by it to a beautiful lagoon, and I rested there refreshed, excited, and at peace, knowing that the current was there to carry me whenever I was ready!"

The fourth one says:

"We had met and were friends at once, she and I. We talked of many things—of art, of music, and of philosophy. There was more than a tiny tingle in this experience—a tingle which presaged what was to come. But I was not ready. I was not together. Who knows if she was or not?

"We ate, we danced, we even got tired together. We touched in a cursory way and were gentle and loving. But we did not love.

"Our relationship grew. And as it grew, it broke on the rocks of fear, demand, and control and ran aground in the sticky mud of mutual projection.

"We parted, we left, we said a not-so-angry goodbye. There were tears in the eye and a catch in the throat. But still no flow of emotion to carry us on. So we went our ways.

"Then one day it happened. I saw her in a vision, in a fantasy. I had made these fantasies before but this one caught me by the balls and carried me in its power. I called, I went to her, I threw myself into her abyss. She might be controlling me, but I didn't care.

"She was coy and seemingly cold as she fended me off. But I could see the pulsating in her body as we sat fully clothed barely touching. I knew all too well the tingling electricity in mine. It flowed back and forth in me like the waves pounding again and again against a rocky shore. And she found it difficult to sit still when I looked through her and plumbed the depths of her soul.

"We moved to seclusion. We faced each other at last. As we approached, my ears pounded like the giant tympany of a huge primitive orchestra. We touched and the heat arose. We were carried along by a giant undulating current. The current grew hotter, more fiery. We melted but we did not flow together. We penetrated, we encountered, we blended our separate rhythms into one. Our electricity sparkled and cracked, as it formed a huge glowing ball which enveloped us. We were together but still separate. Our two trips were moving in separate rhythms, which interpenetrated and formed a greater enveloping rhythm. The lightning struck in blinding strokes again and again. We were still each his own and climbing, rising, flying up the elevator of each other. Then the lightning flashed in one ecstatic stroke. The cable broke. And we melted and flowed together in one pulsating, breathing stream. But it was not over. We had found a resting place beside a beautiful reflecting marble pool where we could collect our oneness. We were together—I with her and she with me—and we were part of the universe and all eternity!"

There are many things that these four peaks have in common. A feeling of a movement, energy, and motivation that transcends the person and seems to come from elsewhere. A feeling of power and confidence, the ability to cope with whatever happens. A feeling of unity, identity, wholenesss, "I am one, I am together, and I know who I am!" A feeling of craziness, madness, dizziness which is not like the usual everyday experiences. A feeling of daring, risking, intentionally throwing aside ordinary controls. A feeling of short time span, that the experience of the peak is momentary, but that its effect is lasting. We are nurtured on the belief that we can scale the peak again at will. A feeling of wonder and delight—we do not understand it fully ever, how it came or where it went. But we are delighted and fascinated by it.

How does one scale the peak? How do we induce peak experiences in our lives? This is more difficult to say. But we can say that peaks only come to us when we are together—when we are together *in* body and *with* our body. Peaks are essentially, but not only, feeling experiences. And a split body, or person, cannot scale a peak. The split person would hold back or be in doubt which peak to scale and would never get there. Furthermore the split person would be afraid to let go of controls. He would be using too much energy to keep apart the two sides of his split, fearing to let them come together because he fears the intensity of a totally unified experience. Peaks, then, are for those who are together. Valleys for those who are split and apart.

28

What about plateaus? They may seem to be in between the peaks and valleys, but are they? Here again let us let those who experience plateaus speak. The first speaker says:

"My life is generally very good. My wife and I have had fifteen years of marriage and three wonderful children. I have a good job. I am an engineer and have been treated well by my company. I get three weeks of vacation each year and I certainly look forward to it. Next year we plan to take our camper and spend quite a while going up the coast to the Pacific Northwest.

"I haven't had many promotions or salary raises lately— defense spending is off in our area and I am just glad not to be laid off.

"What do I do with my spare time? I read the daily papers and my favorite magazines. The wife and kids watch TV, but I only watch it when a big football game is on, or the World Series. Occasionally I will read a popular novel or autobiography.

"We enjoy our friends. Bill and Edna are our closest. My wife, Virginia, is always on the phone with Edna, and we enjoy going on weekend outings together with our children—our three and their two.

"No, we don't go to many plays or shows, unless it is a benefit for my service club. We stay at home a good bit. On weekends I have work to do around the house and yard. Never have gotten that brick patio finished. Occasionally we may go to a neighborhood movie, but they have really been lousy lately!

"All in all its a good life, though. I pay my bills. We generally stay well—except for the surgery Virginia had last year and my ulcer the year before. Kids are getting older now and we must send them through college. So we can't be banging around the country spending money like we did when we were single. Of course, when they are through college we'll really have our fling. When will that be? About ten or twelve years until Jimmy, our youngest, gets out of college. That will be our silver wedding anniversary. Plenty of time for a fling after that."

A second speaker says:

"I'm an executive secretary for Mr. James P. Finch, Senior partner of Finch, Lynch, Levering, architectural consultants. I am well paid, and I have great respect and admiration for my boss. I have been with this firm for twelve years. I started as one of the secretarial staff, but I became so interested in the company that they gave me several promotions and raises. Somehow Mr. Finch noticed me after I had been with F., L., and L. only two years. And he selected me to be his personal assistant with the title of executive secretary.

"What do I do in my job? Well, in a sense, I am Mr. Finch's office wife. Yes, of course he is married! He has a lovely wife and two outstanding children. And I respect Mrs. Finch very much—although lately she does seem a bit cold and aloof when she comes to the office. I take care of all the little details of office management which are so necessary to keep it running smoothly just as a wife does in the home. I do admire Mr. Finch so much, and I hate to see him discouraged or upset about a problem or a sticky detail. So I consider it only fair for me to relieve him of all unnecessary concerns—even to staying over and working extra hours when necessary.

"No, you are *absolutely* wrong! There is no emotional involvement between me and Mr. Finch. I am an office wife in the job sense *only*. I am sure he appreciates my work and my loyalty. And I have never had a boss who is as kind and considerate. But this is as far as our relationship goes.

"My social life? Well I don't really have time for very much. I work quite long hours. I have to be on call whenever the firm enters into a new contract, and there seem to be a lot of them lately. I do play a little golf and I love to go to the beach and relax when I have a chance. Then, too, I am always reading up on the newer developments in architecture. Just finished a new biography of Frank Lloyd Wright. I have a very good girl friend who is a social worker. We occasionally go to a play together, but lately our schedules don't seem to dovetail too well. Maybe we can go on a trip together when I get my summer vacation. I'll have to ask Mr. Finch when would be the best time for me to be away."

And now a third speaker:

"I am a professor of history at the State University. I have been on the faculty for ten years and am quite satisfied with my job. We have received regular raises in pay until recently. But before things got tight, I had reached the top of our salary scale so I'm not doing too badly.

"No, I'm not married. I did marry right after I got my degree, when I was still in the East. But that didn't work out too well. She was too young, too much an outdoors girl, too free. We split up after only one year. Since then I have lived alone and I guess that's the way it will stay.

"Oh, yes. I have dates and friends but no involvements for me. I value my style of life too much to let someone else screw it up for me. And I certainly wouldn't want to impose it on anyone else either.

"I spend most of my time professionally. I try to keep my lectures up to date and that takes a good bit of reading. Then, too, I like to publish an article or two every year and there is the book I have been trying to get finished on Thomas Jefferson. In the summer I do travel, mostly in the eastern states. Next year I plan to go to Europe and see some of the glory that used to exist in Greece and Rome. Maybe I will develop a new interest, but I'm not sure."

"But these people don't seem unhappy really," you say. "They may have made a very good adjustment to life and its problems. They may lack a bit of excitement and thrill. But they all seem sure of their life style and what it can give them. They don't seem to get depressed. Their emotional balance seems to be good. Why wouldn't anyone choose to be on a plateau?"

My point here is not to recommend any particular life style. Many of us are continually in the valleys and some who are there undoubtedly could get out if they chose to do so. Others are on emotional plateaus and, as with our three speakers above, see no real reason to change. Still others seek to scale the heights—to sacrifice almost anything to have a peak experience built into their lives. These choices are theirs. Who can say they are wrong?

"But you have said that valleys of feeling are caused by splits in the person, in his body awareness, and between the person and the outside reality. Peaks are experienced by those who are whole and together and secure in themselves. What are the personal qualities of those on the plateaus of feeling?"

Well, the plateau dwellers are those who continually control, plan ahead, avoid risks, rationalize, and sublimate. They have their lives well in order and so can avoid the pitfalls which will cause depression and despair. They often regret and look back to the time when they were single, or look ahead to the time when their children will be through college, as our first plateau couple did. Our professor undoubtedly has regrets about his marriage and also about his future plans to avoid its recurrence. His heavy emphasis on professional matters helps compensate for the lack of other kinds of involvements. Our executive secretary regrets a crowded and full work schedule in a way, but plans to continue it. This will keep her busy and help her to avoid other nonwork involvements with which she might not be able to cope. She is vociferous in her denial of emotional involvement with, or desire for, her boss. A bit too vociferous perhaps. If she works hard enough and long enough for him and his office details, she may be able to handle these camouflaged desires for a long time.

So our plateau dwellers are secure from the attack and sickness of depressions. But they are also relatively sure never to know the peaks. There may have been peaks in their past—scary ones. A marriage with a vibrant young girl. A look of approval from a handsome executive and perhaps an invitation for dinner in a secluded spot. A wild "bang around the country" by a couple before they were married. But now the spontaneity and willingness to throw off all controls is lacking, and their bodies have become necessarily anesthetized in part, so as to squelch and repress certain kinds of feelings which would be too much for them to handle.

"But this sounds a bit like the people of the valley. They lack feelings because they are split and out of touch. The plateau people, you say, are also turned off. How are they different?"

The difference is really a matter of degree—and yet it is more than that. The valley people are *essentially* split and so are. apart from themselves and the world in most of the important dimensions of life. Therefore they see *everything* as depressing and hopeless. The plateau people are in touch with most things, but are anesthetized to certain areas which might produce "dangerous" involvements. They avoid deep involvement *now* and live in the past and future. They have feelings which are deep, but they are related to past or future—*there and then.* In this way they turn off and anesthetize themselves to areas which they feel they cannot handle now. Their feelings are real and they experience them now, but they are not *now feelings.* They relate essentially to *there and then!*

Finally, each of these types of feelings is real. They are experienced typically by different kinds of people. But many of us experience each of them at different times. In subsequent chapters we shall look at some of the techniques for developing and changing from one type of feeling to another. But the essential idea is the movement toward or away from *now* and the value of touch in facilitating this movement.

5

The Paradox
of
Control

When I am controlling, I am not,
When I am not controlling, I am!

"Pamela is an ideal wife. She is always at home. She takes care of the children—feeds them, gets them to school, sees that they don't get into trouble. She keeps the house in apple-pie order. She is a wonderful cook. Whenever I need love, affection, sex, she is always willing. She is ready to go anywhere with me at a moment's notice. And she never complains when I have to work late or go off alone on a business trip. What more could I ask?"

Possible translation:

"Pamela submits completely to my control. She does exactly what I tell her to do and complies exactly with my expectations and requirements of her. There are many things I might like to ask, but not of Pamela. She couldn't come through in those departments."

"Susan is a wonderful girl. She is attractive, intelligent, warm. But lately she has taken to emotional outbursts, tears, anger. I am patient, but I have to use all my strength to get her to control herself. It upsets me to think that these outbursts may continue after we are married. I don't want to be tied to someone who can't get hold of herself! I hope she gets over this weakness soon!"

Possible translation:

"Susan is really not so wonderful. She has a basic defect which bothers me very much. She can't control herself and I can't control her very well either. Unless she changes, I will never marry her. I couldn't live with her as she now is!"

"Bob is my husband and I love him. We have a good marriage in spite of some of his limitations. He never comes home on time, whether it's for dinner or after a business meeting. I often remind him of this, but he doesn't seem to pay any attention to my feelings. Last night, when he was so very late, I made him sleep in the living room on the sofa. Maybe that will make him realize how much I worry when he is late!"

Possible translation:

"Bob is my husband and I'm stuck with him. I have controlled him in most of the areas of life, but he resists my control of his lateness in coming home and also my control of his sexual desires. Last night I locked the bedroom door so he couldn't sleep with me. I really don't enjoy sex with him anyway so I didn't miss him in bed at all. I particularly don't appreciate it when he comes on so strong. My biggest worry is that I can't get control of him. I wonder if he will ever get over his weakness!"

"Jerry is truly a wonderful man. It is amazing how he has changed since we have been going together. He was always thoughtful and considerate of my wishes. And now that he knows more fully what pleases me, it is so much more comforting and exciting to be with him. He dresses in that neat and well-groomed way I have always admired, and he only drinks wine now, no distilled liquor. He may get a glow on at parties, but is never drunk or loud. I feel so proud of him, and I am sure our life together will be a success."

Possible translation:

"Jerry is controllable and I control him! At first he resisted doing what I wanted him to do. But when he found that our arguments over these things spoiled his sex, he saw the light of day. His style of dress and habits of drinking were so gross. Now he follows my suggestions to a T. Since he has changed—and as long as he stays in line—I can live with him. I can control him and everyone knows it too. This pleases me and makes me feel secure. I know where I'm at!"

These four statements and their possible translations speak of control—control of one person by another. Read these statements carefully. After reading each one, read the possible translation. Do these translations seem to be valid interpretations of what the speakers may really have had in mind? If not, make your own translations. Or do you feel that those who make such statements about another person mean just exactly what they say and no more?

The speakers are trying to do what the root meaning of the word "control" suggests—to keep a counter-roll, a copy, a replica of the original. The counter-roll was kept by the "controller" to see that things did not get out of line. Today we spell it "comptroller" but it means the same thing. It is this counter-roll—this copy which the controller uses—which is the *instrument* of control. It is the enforced matching of the copy with the original which is the method of control. In each case it is the original which is important. The copy, the counter-roll, the person or thing which is controlled, has little importance or individuality. It is valuable insofar as it *matches* the original.

When applied to persons, the controller is really saying, "I don't love or value you as you are. I value you only insofar as you match my model of what you should be. If you don't match my model, I can still love or value you if you will change, give up what you are, and become what your *aren't*, namely a copy of something else. I, of course, will select the something else which you are to become."

From the examples above, it might seem as though control operates only between the sexes in marital or near-marital situations. While marriage and control are usually kissin' cousins—if not brothers—under the skin, there are many other areas of life where control of one person by another is very important.

In school the teacher says:

"I am assigning chapter 3 to be read by the end of this week. If you read it well and know the answers, I want you to know you will do well on the test on Friday and I will grade you high. You must also come to class every day—and on time! If you are absent, you must make up what *I* say you have missed. If you are tardy too often, you must be punished. You must talk only when I recognize you, and you must sit respectfully and answer when I call on you!"

Teacher really means:

"I am the controller. I assign the work. You do it. I tell you the answers. You learn them. I reward you or not as I see fit. I tell you when to come, what to say, how to sit, when to speak, what to learn, even how to listen. If you give up your individuality and do all these things, I will reward you well. I will control you and you will have been controlled. My first job as a teacher (?) is to *control* you—control my class. All learning (if any) is secondary to this. If any learning comes from an uncontrolled situation it must be bad!"

At home a mother says:

"I want you children here on time for meals. You must eat what I prepare and not snack in between meals. Keep yourselves clean and neat when you go out, and wash your hands before you eat. Get up on time. Be at school promptly. Study hard and learn what the teacher teaches. Be respectful to your father and me, and I want you to know that above all we love you very much!"

Mother is really saying:

"I need to control you—perhaps for fear you might want to do what I did when I was your age or because I can't control myself. If you conform to what I ask of you and to the pattern of the community, you will be rewarded with success. I cannot accept you as a disobedient child. It upsets me too much. I really don't love you unless I can and do control you. Then I can relax. In order for me to do that, you must give up your individuality in many areas of life. If you do this, I will tell you I love you and this ought to make you happy."

At work the boss says:

"Our company is very interested in the welfare of its employees. If we all work hard, the company will prosper and so will each of you. Therefore, I want you all here at 8:00 A.M. ready to work. If you are sick, call in and let me know. But remember, you have only ten days of sick leave a year. Don't waste materials and don't waste time. You will be paid every Friday unless the checks are held up. In that case, you will get them Monday. Follow our approved methods of operation in the office. If you have any ideas for improvement, submit them to me and I assure you they will be considered. When in doubt, ask me or one of the supervisors for help. In this way you will learn the details of our operation most quickly. We expect you to learn our methods and processes after a reasonable length of time. If your progress is not satisfactory, we will let you know. Whatever criticisms you receive in regard to your work are made only to help improve our overall efficiency!"

The boss means:

"The company controls you. I am the agent of this control. I will brook no interference with overall production. I must control your actions and operations in all of their phases. You must give over your own individuality and subject your immediate needs to those of the company. If you do this quickly enough, you will be maintained as an employee, otherwise, not!"

We must pause here a minute and correct what may be a developing misapprehension. You may say, "None of my associates—male or female—is like the four you described in the beginning of this chapter. And I don't know a teacher, a mother, or a boss of today who speaks or thinks like those you have presented. These are straw men and women!"

Well, perhaps they are not typical. They are not intended to be. They are simply presented as examples of control, of control language, and of the differences between overt statements of control and thoughts about control. You will have to check this against your own experiences and those of your friends. If you want to do this, ask yourself the following questions to check on the degree of control in any one of your interpersonal relationships:

1. To what extent are you—or the other person involved—accepted *as you are?*
2. To what extent must you, or the other person, change according to someone else's pattern of development in order to be acceptable?

3.   Is the relationship reciprocal? Does the degree of control work both ways?
4.   Is the relationship symmetrical? Or does one side prescribe the changes in some areas while the other side prescribed changes in other areas? Is the degree of control on both sides relatively even?
5.   Are the degree, area, and kind of control expressed and discussed openly?
6.   Are those who are involved—controlled and controller—aware of their unexpressed feelings and thoughts about the pattern of control?

If you carry out this activity, please realize that there are no right or wrong, good or bad answers to these questions. Your pattern of control is yours. So be it! But this activity should bring the patterns, area, degree, and kind of control to your awareness. If you are aware of it, you can—potentially, at least—control your pattern of control and of being controlled.

Let us now consider another kind of control:

"My name is Harold. I am not married. I live by myself. My life is very full, although at times I would like more excitement. I get up each morning at seven—rain or shine, work day or holiday. I do my regular routine of exercises—sit-ups, leg raises, push-ups. I pride myself on my body, even though the exercise gets me down at times. Then shower, two soft boiled eggs, dry toast, black coffee. My clothes are all arranged in order in my closet—pants one end, coats and jackets at the other, shirts and sweaters in between. It takes me no time to select my costume and dress. I have half an hour for the paper if it is a work day. If not, I may take 45 minutes. My reading schedule is quite full. I subscribe to six magazines which I read regularly from cover to cover. Then I always have a book I am reading and another one on hand when I finish. I have quite a library and can find each book at a moment's notice.

"At work I am very efficient. I am rarely sick—except when I had those sinus headaches last year. My stomach is delicate. But I have learned to eschew heavy and highly seasoned food. Alcohol? Only a glass or two of wine. Can't remember when I was drunk. Back in college, I guess. Or was it New Year's Eve eight years ago?

39

"Companions? Yes I have many friends. But I am careful not to get too close to them, especially to women. I have learned that if involvement seems imminent, I can always retreat. It is a bit tough, but I have learned that this is the best way.

"Money? I have enough. Make a good salary and I have no dependents since my mother died five years ago. I have trained myself to put a fourth of my pay check in the bank or in stocks each month. I am accumulating a bit, and also this pays for my summer trips and my skiing. Yes, I love skiing! Usually go to June Lake but sometime I hope to do my thing in Europe. I will have saved enough by the year after next.

"Entertainment? I go to the symphony concerts occasionally but so often the dates interfere with my reading, my writing (I keep in touch by mail with nearly all my friends), or my other activities at home. You see I like to take care of my house. No one could *ever* do it to my satisfaction!

"On the whole my life is mild, but full—full of details which I enjoy taking care of. Then, too, when I am busy, I never get lonely!"

Could Harold ever let go to himself? If so he might say:

"I'm so fed up with my routine I could *scream*! Those exercises—I'm afraid to stop them. I remember my father's pot-belly. Ugh! I *am* lonely, but I'm afraid of people. I couldn't cope with involvement—male or female. Intense emotions break me up! But how I would love something really *thrilling*! Even my skiing is only on tame slopes. If the truth be known, it's the clothes and the getting away that pleases me. I would love to be downright irresponsible—but that would be terrible! I might stay that way. I guess I'd better just keep myself within bounds and go along as I am!"

"My name is Louise. I work in an office downtown. I was a teacher once—third grade—but I couldn't stand it. I'm disorderly myself and all those kids running around just about did me in! Now I'm a copy writer for an advertising firm. It's a pretty good job, but I can't seem to get hold of myself—can't seem to get on top of the details of the job. I've been there five years, but I always seem to make mistakes. And when I do I feel simply *horrible*! Just like when I overdraw my checking account. Each time I write a check I get the wheemies for fear I will make an error in entering it. And I usually do at least once every other month.

"I have lots of friends—some from way back in college days. And we see each other often. But I'm kind of the laughing stock of the crowd. I'm always late. Never can seem to get off the phone in time to take my shower. And I usually forget my car keys or license, or glasses, or something and have to go back for them. I feel so embarrassed when that happens. Do they ever make fun of me! Sometimes I get really mad at them *inside* when they make fun of me. But I *never* let them know how I feel. Why? They probably wouldn't like me. Good old Louise is their goat—even when she is late and holds everybody up.

"I wish I could get control of myself. I try and try, but self-discipline was always my downfall. My father used to say, 'Louise you'll never get it right. Just do the opposite of what you think! Why must I have a daughter who is so scatterbrained?"

"So I go along my way. All I can seem to do is hold myself back from getting into some really bad mess. Maybe I'll really do *that* some time! I have the most horrible dreams of trying to straighten things out. Can't seem to do it even in a dream!"

Louise seems to be more on the surface than Harold. But is she? Could you ever imagine her thinking to herself:

"I hate being made fun of! I hate all those supposed friends who do it! I hate being confused and awkward! Most of all I hate my father and all his perfectly disciplined crap! I'm tired of trying to be orderly and controlled and always failing at it! I wish *just once* I could *intentionally* make a mess—a hell of a mess—and brag about it. That would be heaven! But I *wouldn't* dare! I'd lose all my friends. And my family wouldn't be able to stand it. So I just have to go on making a mess of things, but trying like hell not to.

Louise and Harold are controllers too—like the spouses of Pamela, Susan, Bob, and Jerry—but in the cases of Louise and Harold the object of their control is themselves, not someone else. Nevertheless the process is quite similar. There is the counter-roll, the copy, which must be matched with the original, the model. In this case, however, Louise and Harold are both the controller and the controlled. They have in their "minds" a model which they have introjected—swallowed whole—without knowing what it really means or how it would affect their lives. They then attempt to match themselves against this model. Harold seems to be more successful on the surface. He seems to be able to make the *surface* of his life match the model of perfect order, in the physical as well as in the emotional dimensions of his life. Louise works at the job as hard as Harold, but always mucks it up. I would be hard to tell without more clinical data which one is under the greater pressure of control.

We have now covered many of the kinds of control—perhaps the most important ones. In each of these there is a push, exerted by some person. And there is the resistance of the one who is controlled or who is to be controlled. It is at this point that the paradox of control arises. For when I push on you—Pamela, Susan, Bob, Jerry, student, child, employee, Louise, or Harold—you necessarily resist my control. The harder I pressure you, the harder you resist. I may temporarily squelch or anesthetize you, so that your so-called "stubborn" behavior is not in evidence to me. Therefore I may see you as controlled, and you may feel controlled. However that which is squelched is not dead, and as energy it *cannot* be destroyed. Hence it will be bound to show its effect somewhere else, often in the most unexpected place. Pamela, the perfect wife, may start drinking to relieve her tensions and end up as an alcoholic. Susan, the attractive bride-to-be, may be in line for a hysterectomy—particularly if her outbursts are "cured." Bob, the loving but tardy husband, may develop an ulcer—or a girl friend at his office. Jerry, the well-groomed boy friend, may develop a form of sexual impotence. Students are likely to be chronically sick or absent. Children may become destructive of property instead of striking back at parents. And employees may develop all kinds of accidents on the job. These are only suggestions of ways in which the supposedly controlled person manifests his resentment of the attempt to control him and shows *indirectly* how the control has misfired. These side effects of the *attempt* to control are often entirely unconscious as far as the controlled person is concerned. Hence, Harold does not see that headaches and a delicate stomach may be a resistance to self-control. And Louise does not see that her errors, too, can be the result of compulsive attempts to force herself *never* to make *any* errors in anything! Hence the first half of the paradox, "When I am controlling, I am not". In any *total* sense, the attempt to suppress behavior by only the act of an ego—one's own or another's—results in displaced behavior. And since the direction and nature of the displacement is unpredictable, it cannot be controlled in any predetermined way. We can never tell just what Pamela or Harold will do when suppressed. It is beside the point as to whether it is ever justified to ask or demand that anyone give up the individuality necessary to fit the "counter-roll."

But suppose, now, that I decide that the giving up of individuality is not desirable—that, in fact, individuality is a God-like trait and should not be violated under any condition? Then, Pamela, you should be encouraged to flower in a new direction. Perhaps you should start to paint, to forget to get dinner on occasion, and to hire a baby-sitter so that you can go to that art class at the University. Maybe you might even dare to stay home and paint the beautiful ocean by the moonlight rather than go to that convention in Chicago with your husband.

And Bob, perhaps you need to take a trip to the mountains by yourself—not even inviting your wife at all. Perhaps you need to have some specific joy in your life so that if you are late, it will be for a purpose. Perhaps, wife, you might encourage him in this and tell him that he is welcome whenever he comes home. Then, perhaps, Bob will be a real man on his own, an individual, and not just a husband badly melting into that mold called "home!"

Susan, why are emotional outbursts so bad, so destructive? Must you always be calm and cool? And my dear fiance, do you not want the heat of passion in Susan, your wife-to-be? Then why not try letting her have her outbursts and carry them to the peak—to their conclusion? Susan may become far more relaxed and your sex life may be improved immeasurably!

Jerry, you *are* a paragon of virtue. You are almost a "mother's little boy." Don't you feel you need some balls? Go out and buy a green and purple polka dot shirt and let your beard grow. And after you have had a good blast of scotch, sit down and talk to your lady love. I'm sure if she really wants *you*, she may see that while her feelings and preferences are hers and deserve to be expressed, she will not want them to cut off your individuality. You can learn a great deal from her tastes and her preferences. But the decisions about your personal habits must be yours—and she will learn to love you that way if she really wants *you*!

And you—teacher, mother, boss—you might be cultivators and lovers of individuality instead of sacrificers of it on the altar of your insecurity! Teacher, you might give back to your students the gift of refusal, of denial, of self-assertion. You might let them do, think, and act as they feel, not as you think they *should* feel! Why do I need the *right* answer, *your* right answer? What is so heinous about absence and tardiness? Is your class room a temple? What a thrilling experience to be allowed to be wrong once in a while! Perhaps if I want to be strong, I must risk being wrong!

Mother, your children are dear to you. Can you stand to let them be different from you? To disobey you? To occasionally be ill-humored and downright disrespectful? Do *you* ever feel this way? Well, so do they. And the whipping post of punctual performance according to your plan is most disrespectful of their individuality.

And dear employer—boss, as you are usually called—do you *really* want the best from your employees? Is the company *really* interested in their welfare? If so, you will not violate their most cherished possession. You will be less concerned with waste of materials and time and more concerned with wasting the creativity of your men, which is the greatest gift they have to give you. Give them personal security, give them respect, give them a chance to be original and perhaps differ with your procedures, and your company will soar to the heights on the wings of their creative interest. Any machine, any mule, any robot or computer can be on time and faultless in following you!

What can we say to Harold and Louise? Only that you both are in a double bind. You are both controller and controlled. Let up! Let up! Flow! Melt! Do you have to be perfect, and hard? Do you have to be forever struggling and chasing to control yourselves? Can you, by chance, look at yourselves more carefully—more humanly? Can you be more accepting of what you see? Can you let up with your becoming, with your achieving, and just BE? If so, a new world might open to you. And the center of that world would be your existence *now!*

"But," I hear you say, "you are trying to exhort me to be good and to fit into *your* plan. Yours is only a slightly veiled way of controlling. You are pressing and promoting individuality and personal creativity. 'Down with suppression and imposed control!' You would like to push me into your mold, wouldn't you? Suppose I choose and like to be controlled, what then? Suppose I see imposed control as the only way we weak and fallible human beings can get along?"

"Well, of course that is your privilege, your choice, and your problem. How you will deal with the unpredictability of displaced behavior, I do not know. Maybe you will say, "Take each act and each item by itself and you can control the whole." But what happens when your displacements become so numerous and repeated that they take over, as often happens in times of economic and social crisis? Or in adolescence and at other times of personal crisis? It is your problem to work out. No exhortation on my part can, or should, convince or control you. Only *your own* experience can really control you. Why not choose this as your guide?

This brings us to the other side of the paradox, "When I am not controlling, I am." But first, how about a dash—or just a pinch—of philosophy?

We have said, "When I am controlling, I am not." Did I hear you say, "I am not *what*?" If so, perhaps you answered yourself, "I am not *controlling*! of course." And you would be right. When I try to control you by pushing you or try to control me by pushing me, it backfires. You backfire! I backfire! So I am not controlling, just pushing!

But that isn't all. What is an even more powerful idea is that when I—this individual person—become, or make myself, a controller, I not only destroy your individuality but I destroy mine as well. This is because the only individuality that I *can* clearly see in you is *mine*—my own individuality. I see the me in you. In this sense when I want to control your alcoholic tendencies, am I not trying to control those alcoholic tendencies which I feel I would have if I were in your situation? When mother wants to control daughter's curfew time, is she not seeking to control what she, mother, thinks she would feel and do if she were in daughter's situation? If so, the controller is controlling himself *in the other person*, and correspondingly denying and destroying his own individuality. When he is *controlling* himself, he is not *being* himself. Therefore, the controller is no longer an "I", he *is not!* Insofar as he continues to be a controller, he ceases to exist as an

"I." When I am controlling (am a controller) I *am not*, for I have denied myself.

Now back to the other side again. What happens when I am *not* controlling? What *do* I do? What and how do I feel? If I am in a close personal relationship and am *not* controlling my partner, nor trying to control him, nor even putting *myself* in a psychological corset, then I must be together. I must be secure. I must be in touch with reality. I must know what is going on in me—and you. I will probably feel alive and excited at the new things that I continually feel growing in me, and the new things that I am continually aware of blossoming in you. I will seek to cultivate all of this newness. If you strike out at me or threaten me, I may duck and say, "Ouch, that hurts!" But I will not deny it, squelch it, or damn it. I will seek to concentrate on the feeling that this "blow" creates in me—or rather I will seek to be aware of how I make myself feel when you strike out (or so it seems to me)—at me. I will not try to analyze your reasons for what you do. I will avoid projecting my feelings on to you, and if I do project, I will label it so. In such a case, I am being me and trying to let you be fully you in all the many colors which your personality affords.

If I have been away from you and am about to see you again, I will undoubtedly have some expectations regarding your behavior, appearance, mood, etc. When I do see you—whether you are my lover, wife, mother, teacher, boss, or friend—I will take what you give me. If you are surly or ill-tempered (or so it seems to me) I will not offer to help or change you. I will greet you as usual and perhaps comment on your appearance. I may also tell you of my feelings if I have any I want to share. "Hello, Joe. That's a neat shirt you have on. Don't believe I've seen it before. I feel lousy today. Too many beers last night. I'd like to talk with you about that new contract if you have time later on!" Or, "Good morning, Darling. That was a beautiful evening last night! I love you in that dress. It's such a good fit. Would you like to go to lunch at the Bayside Inn today? Don't feel well? Well, we can make it another time! I want to hear about that new book you are reading when you have a chance."

When you are gentle, loving, warm, and appreciative in a myriad of new ways, I will love each one of them *now*. I will make no recriminations concerning why you don't do this more often, or analyze why or when this beautiful newness came. I will accept it, love it, and praise it. It is mine now. I will let it grow as it will. I will let it—let you—unfold according to your own unpredictable pattern.

Whenever your companion's mood is positive, cheery, supportive, there is *supposed* to be no problem. But here the tendency is to take it all for granted, assuming this is the way your companion always should be. "Well, it's good to see you happy again." Or, "Thank God the storm clouds are passed. I wish we could work together like this all the time." Such statements immediately control by comparison with the model of the past or with what you like in the future.

On the other hand, to keep the relationship together, I must relate to you in the present. I must be aware and communicate to you what *I* am aware of now. And I must not invade your privacy either. One of the greatest forms of control is the control of mutual confession—particularly when the desire for the confession isn't mutual. I control you by telling you *all* about me and expecting (insisting?) that you do the same. We see, then, that the noncontrolling relationship must be reciprocal, accepting, and not judgmental. It is a two-way street for each. But it can never be symmetrical. No two plants or organisms of any kind can grow together as mirror images of each other!

In the case of myself—of self-control—the problem is more complicated because of the double bind mentioned before. I am controller and controlled. In a noncontrolling relationship with myself, I must do just as I would with anyone else whom I don't want to control—accept me, accept myself as I am. Take my bad moods with the good. Don't pass judgments on me. Try not to squelch any mood. Don't wait anxiously for someone or something else to "cheer me up." Try not to do the comparison thing with my past or future moods. "God, how terrible it will be in that new town I am moving to! No friends! No familiar places!" Or, "How I wish I were back in good old Gladsville. There I really lived! I sure get myself in a lot of messes that make me move away. I wish I were more careful!" It is such put downs of myself which I must avoid if I want to grow out of my self-controlling patterns. If I am aware of me and accept me, then what I do and whatever happens is acceptable, and does not need to be put down. I will not always be happy. But then, the sun doesn't shine every hour of every day. Why should it? Just as I accept night as well as day and clouds as well as sun, so I accept my moods of despair, happiness, sorrow, and joy.

"But all of this is not control! It is just awareness and acceptance. How can you possibly call this control at all! And how can a life be lived with no direction, no rudder, no guiding star?"

That's just the point of the second half of the paradox. There is no *external* control, no *planned* control. But there is an inner control, a spontaneous control. So if I throw away my conscious desire to control myself or another, I am turning my ego off and just relaxing and letting things happen. My desire is to be interested, attentive, alive, and fascinated by the multitude of experiences which flow by and through me. I am aware of the flow of experience as though it were a river. It has a direction. It is *my* experience. It is me. Therefore I have a flow, a direction. The flow develops its guide as it moves on, just as a child does in a toy box, or as a dream does as it unfolds. I—my ego—does not need to *give* a direction to the stream or to me. Of course occasionally there will be rocks in the stream as well as places where the flow is more beneficial to my trip. Here my ego and my subconscious and my other subpersonalities (if you prefer these terms) will be internally organized, so that I flow with maximum effectiveness. If I capsize, I get a cool bath and start again. It is no tragedy. But I cannot push the river. If I try, I will only dam it up, and the flow will gradually reduce amd ultimately cease, and that which is of value in me—my flow, my life, my individuality—will die!

If this is true of me, it is also true of my partner, my family, my associates, at work or at play. They, too, have a flow which is uniquely theirs. To dam it is to kill it. To control it is to dam it. We can flow together—if we don't insist on being completely merged into one. We can be together as long as we both recognize that our flows are different—desirably different. As soon as we try to merge our two flows into one, we are no longer together, because we have lost the individuality which makes together possible. We become, then, a sluggish stream, a shallow lake, a marsh, a swamp. And our flow becomes stagnant, full of sediment, and overgrown with mold and toxic vegetation. We must be somewhat separate and distinctly unique to be and flow freely and freshly together. If we come together in this way, it is beautiful. If we do not, no power on earth could make it so. It could only control us, dam us, stop our flow, and so kill us.

Perhaps another analogy will help here. If we are dancing together in the contemporary style, we are not merged into one. We are still individual persons dancing together. You do not tell me what to do, nor I you. We follow each other—each one alternately initiating movements and rhythms and responding to the other. We respond to, but do not copy, the beat of the music nor do we *exactly* copy each other. We dance variations around the musical beat. I dance variations of your movements. And you dance variations of mine. The whole dance experience has an inner control which emerges as we proceed. No one could predict exactly what we would do or how we would move, before the dancing started, or even before it was over. The inner control of the dance emerges and becomes observable as the dance progesses. We warm up to it, and as we do, we are stimulated and refreshed due to the release which is produced.

I can be this way in all the activities of my life if I choose. If I gradually move into an activity—be it reading, swimming, eating, or sexual intercourse—an inner self may develop (or I may develop an awareness of my inner self?) which will progressively take over and unify all the diverse personalities in me which may want to take over individually and compete for the command of the activity. This inner self unifies *me* and all these diverse elements in me and allows me to flow easily and freely.

When I join with you in an activity, our two inner selves form a higher union which again unifies *us* and allows us to flow together, provided that you, too, have your inner self in working order. In this way we learn to flow together by inner control. And we do this in an unplanned and unpremeditated way.

"But not planning ahead bothers me. How can you live safely, securely, and never plan, just flow?"

Who said living was safe or secure? It is, and must be, a gamble. There are dangers, so-called, at every bend in the stream. Someone may have polluted the stream or dammed it. There may be floods or treacherous currents. But if one has lived fully, with a variety of currents, the course of the stream gets more exciting and less threatening with each mile. Security comes from being able to take the current *right now*—just as it is—and to put my confidence in the flow, and from being able to deal with the fullness and the excitement of the flow as well as with the shallow places and the rocks. Such security develops in me if I am in touch with my inner self. I then *feel* the unity which this inner self produces in me.

49

Of course, occasionally my glance will take in the vista of the stream ahead as well as the beauties I have negotiated behind. This will heighten my appreciation of what is at hand by broadening my view. But I am always with what is now. Even when I am looking back or ahead it is for now that I do it! And I am always in touch with my inner self now.

"Do you call this control? You said by doing this you *are*. I assume you meant, 'When I am not controlling (when I am flowing), I *am*—controlling?' "

In a way you are right. Flowing is not ego controlling—not always and continuously watching what is happening. At most the flowing person is only occasionally watching in a conscious sense. His ego is at best watching with one eye, as it were. But he is in touch with his inner self. And this inner self is making it possible for him to flow and feel the inner security of a unified self—a self in which all the subpersonalities are organized and cooperating in the flow.

If I want to flow in this way, it is true that I must do something to get with, get into, the flow—and I consciously do this. I provide opportunities so that I can sense and experience life more and more fully—so that I can be more in touch with my inner self. But in the ordinary sense of conscious ego control, I am *not* controlling. When I flow, however, I *do* control. For I, as a total being, as an inner self, conscious and subconscious, body and mind, am *in* control. But I, as an ego, am *out of* conscious control per se. I am not pushing. But I am far more fully in control because all of the facets of *me* are in cooperation. I, together, am controlling, in the sense of flowing. I am controlling in the sense that my dreams flow out as a result of some kind of design, albeit not a predetermined one. Maybe that's the key. Flowing is moving and living without predetermined control—by self or by others. But it is a far more immediate and complete kind of control because it operates *now*—when it is needed—and because it involves all of me.

The paradox may now be translated as follows: "When I am pressing with my ego to control, my pressure backfires and there is no inner control—no unified control. For this reason I, as a unified person, *do not* exist. I am *not*. When I give up my ego control, I allow myself to become more totally unified. I may then get more in touch with my inner self and may develop a far more unified form of control. At such times I, as a unified person, *do* exist. Therefore, I am."

Can you see, now, that when I am *not* controlling, in the ego, predetermined sense, I, as my inner self, am really controlling more fully? But much more than this, when I am flowing in this non ego type of control, I, as a person, am much more fully me! I *am* more fully together. I *am* more fully now. I *am*! To lose control is to gain it—and the *it* which I gain is my awareness of my inner self.

> *Control by ego muscle splits me wide.*
> *It fails its purpose, leaves my self denied.*
> *Control from inner self is full and free.*
> *It does the job, makes me more fully me!*

6

Losing Control,
Riding With Feelings

"I felt like my head was going to split wide open. I couldn't take it any more, so I went for a couple of aspirins. What do you take? I seem to need aspirin more and more lately."

"When I came home, I found all those bills in the mail and the third notice on my house mortgage. Then came that phone call. He couldn't make it tonight—after I had gotten that new dress and done everything I could think of to please him! Well, I was just done in! I kept that dress on and headed for Mary's house. Thank God she always has an ear for me! She sure knows how to put my head straight about men. In a half hour or so—after a few drinks—I was myself again and ready to face the world. I don't know what I would do without a friend like her!"

"Last Friday when I got home, I was a bundle of nerves. Everyone seemed to jump on me at the office all day long. Then on the way home it was bumper to bumper on the freeway. When I pulled into my driveway, I was shaking all over. I tried to settle it with some soothing music on the stereo, but the telephone kept up an incessant jangling. I had no other choice but to dig out a couple of tranquilizers. Then I could relax and see things calmly."

"That salad was simply delicious—crisp fresh lettuce, radishes, sliced cucumber, carrots, cherry tomatoes—all the ingredients I love. And the dressing was a work of art—very bland with a piquant taste of delicate herbs in the background, so that the flavor of each vegetable was brought out and not camouflaged. But after dinner my digestive apparatus was really upset. I had to stay within close reach of the bathroom. Almost had to cancel my evening meeting. Only thing that saved me was that syrup I always take for my colitis, and a quart of buttermilk I had on hand. Wonder why good things upset me so much? Wish I could get my gut in better shape."

"My head was stopped up and my throat was sore. My eyes were heavy and my forehead was getting hot as fire. I could feel the alternations of chills and hot flashes. I knew I had it but what could I do now? I did not want to let the fever get too high. So I drank lots of cold liquids, bathed my face in cold water, and took some of that fever-killing medicine I always keep on hand. That seemed to do it. But my lethargy and weakness persisted for several days."

"When she wasn't home by midnight, I started to worry mildly. When I had no call by 1:00A.M., I began reviewing all the possibilities. She had never been this late, particularly on a school night. The more I reviewed, the more worried I became. 'I know she is all right,' I told myself. But I just couldn't make it stick. I paced the floor. I turned on the radio. I tried to read. At the sound of each car or each imagined step outside, I jumped to see what it was. A wrong number on the telephone almost blew my mind. Finally I couldn't stand it any longer. I went next door to my neighbor, the mother of three children. There I was calmed by her confident assurance. While we were talking, a car pulled into our driveway and it was Laurie. My worrying for that night was over, thank God! But do I always have to worry like that?"

Each of the six persons above is battling with a problem of control. For some it seems to be almost entirely a bodily thing—headache, digestive tract, fever. For others it is less body and more psyche—nervousness, worry, anger, and depression. In all six cases these phenomena seem to be recurrent. In most of the cases the lack of control seems to be very nearly incapacitating. None of the persons seems able to deal with the situation at hand by himself. Therefore they all find it necessary to call on some outside agent to help them gain control. In some cases the outside agent is a person. In others it is a chemical agent—medicine, food, or stimulant.

What will these six persons do if, and when, the problem recurs? Of course we do not know for sure, but from their statements one could infer that the same "cure" will be called on again. As with the first person who says, "I seem to need aspirin more and more lately," the cure will probably be used even more frequently. If aspirin has stopped my pain before, I am likely to be more ready to take it again when the pain recurs. I do not recognize the headache as a sign of something else going on in me—something I might very well want to know about if I were interested in knowing me more fully. But when I treat the symptom—the headache—I act as though that is *all* there is to know. And so I split off my knowledge of this other part of myself. When I split myself in this way I become an easy prey of the aspirin. And so I become "hooked" on it. Instead of my controlling my headache, it is the aspirin which *controls me!* And this could apply to any of the other five curative agents mentioned above.

"You mean I can get 'hooked' on friendship or neighborliness? This does not seem to make sense! Isn't it the kindness and the help of other people that makes life worth living? Don't we need even *more* of these qualities? How could one ever have too much of human warmth?"

It all depends on what I want my life to be—how I want to live it. If I want to grow toward taking more responsibility for my actions, feelings, thoughts, and emotions, then this means that external agents must be *called on* only in drastic situations and these should occur less and less frequently. It is one thing to have warm sympathetic persons in my life. It is quite another to feel that without these people I could not get along. It is one thing to have a warm touch or a kind word. It is quite different to look for, to expect, to feel the need of these touches and words whenever a difficult situation or crisis faces me. The first is a gratefully accepted bonus. The second becomes a crutch and a handicap in my becoming more responsible for myself. If undue reliance on aspirin or alcohol is such a crutch, so is undue reliance on people, food, or medicine. I can be hooked on friendship or neighborliness to the extent that I cannot do without them, and to the extent that they keep me from knowing myself more deeply and fully.

"But what can I do when I am suffering from great pain, sorrow, worry, nervousness, etc., except to "kill" the discomfort somehow? Must I suffer needlessly? If I know a remedy, why not use it?"

The man in chapter 2 (p. 7) was faced with this same problem. The problem is that the remedy is not really a remedy at all. As we said before, it is the treatment of a superficial symptom and, as such, blocks deeper knowledge of what is really going on. Each of the six persons with whom we started this chapter were suffering. They wanted to end, or escape from, their suffering. But did they want *just* a temporary relief? I believe not. They expressed at least mild concern about their dependence on the "remedy." I believe they would prefer a more permanent cure. But all they know is the temporary one. Their reluctance to run to it immediately shows at least some desire to escape and be independent of the remedy. And they perhaps know—or intuitively *feel*—that the remedy will not work in the long run. They have known alcoholics, medicine addicts, even sympathy addicts. They do not want this. At best they will rationalize that their "addiction" is the only way out. And for them it may be, unless they want to experience great pain. But they know the remedy does not cure, it only temporarily deadens. Even the person with the fever, who is taking probably the most generally accepted remedy, suffers from "lethargy and weakness" as a result. Is this caused by the fever, or by the cure?

"So my remedy is not a cure! Well I know it isn't a permanent one. But what else can I do? When it gets so bad I have to do something! I can't control it by myself!"

You are quite right. You have to do something. But have you ever thought of going *with* your problem—*into* your pain—instead of *against* it or *out* of it? You can't control it because you don't really know it. You don't accept it as a part of you. This is emphasized by the fact that you refer to your pain—your problem—as "it." You say you can't control *it*. Really you need to control *you*. If you would say, "I can't control me by myself," you might realize what the problem is a bit more clearly. If I can't control *me*, that implies that there are two of me—and that they are not in agreement. My control is deficient because I am split, not together. If I could heal the split and become whole, my control problem would be greatly reduced or vanish entirely.

"But what is this split? What are the two parts of me? And how do I go about healing the split? What can I do?"

No one else can tell you what your split is or what are the two parts of it. You can do it, if you want to—if you can stand to go *into* the pain of your control problem. Here are a few possibilities.

If you have a headache, try riding with it instead of squelching it or pushing it away or anesthetizing yourself. When you anesthetize yourself, you tend to make the split more permanent. When you are in this condition you are not aware of the split. But it is still there— witness the fact that when the aspirin wears off, you still have the headache. But under anesthesia you cannot *work at* the split at all. Therefore it gets more and more established and will need repeated treatments.

If you stop controlling, squelching, or killing the ache, you can feel it more acutely. If you will then turn your full attention to it, you can locate it exactly in your body, see just where it is in your head. You can see how it throbs, how the beat of it changes, how it moves (if it does) to other parts of your head, neck, perhaps shoulders. As you follow it— follow *you*—you get to know it and accept it as part of you. It is no longer *it*. It is you! You own it. You begin to understand it. As this happens, the split starts to heal and the ache may tell you of other things which are associated with it. You may even get an insight as to where it comes from. Perhaps some previously repressed feeling may come to the surface of your attention. At this point the parts of the split may become clear to you and you may see exactly what they are.

You may see one part of you wanting to express the repressed feeling. You may see another part wanting to squelch this feeling and repress it. You may also become aware that there is an inner self which may be called on to help heal the split. This is a higher self in the sense that it can be an objective mediator between the two "persons" of the split. This awareness can only come to you if you follow and go into your ache and allow it to live and be you! This, of course, will be painful—perhaps excruciatingly so. But your head will not break. And as you go with this ache, you have the satisfaction of knowing how to deal with it—with *you*—directly. Your inner self is in control, and you are not pushing. You are simply riding with the feeling and letting it—letting you—take you where you will! The ego of you—the pusher—has lost control, has been united with the rest of you, and is riding out the feeling wherever it goes. If you do this, you will be purged of the division which is splitting you—the division between your ego and the passive part of you. It will be washed out by the flow of pain and feeling which you have experienced. It will be healed by your inner self. And you will be more one, more whole, more together!

"Ok, I see how I can go into a headache, or a physical pain, but what about my psychological pains and upsets—my worry, my nervousness, my attacks of great depression and despondency. What can I do about them, other than to escape and anesthetize? You say I should go with the headache, but my emotional states seem to grow without limit if I do not suppress them. I get terrified of what will happen to me. I am afraid I will crack up, fall apart, go off my rocker! I can't afford to stand or ride with these feelings, can I?"

Well, of course, I don't know what you *want* to stand. But I am relatively sure you *can* stand whatever you *want* to stand. Worry, nervousness, and depression *are* very painful. I am sure that as you concentrate on them they do grow. But undoubtedly you have never let them go far enough. Perhaps it is a crack-up, a falling apart, of your rigid mechanisms of self-control—pure ego control, that is—which is most needed. You sound as though you have yourself in a straight jacket of control. Part of you is struggling to be free—to express itself (yourself). Another part is the controller, the straightjacketer, who pushes and compresses the other you. This battle keeps the two you's apart and split. They never face each other in a fair and equal encounter. And you do not seem to be in touch with your inner self to help negotiate this encounter. It is the controller who fears to let these feelings go. He would not know how to go into partnership with the other you. If you can throw away your escapes and anesthetizers, the underdog "you" will get strong enough to break out and demand a confrontation. If this happens, a working relationship between the two may be negotiated, and your split will be on the road to being healed. This is particularly true if you can get in touch with your inner self to do the negotiating.

However, let's be specific. I am tremendously nervous. What can I do besides take a tranquilizer? Well I can just be nervous. Let my nervousness go, and in the process concentrate on every detail of my nervousness as it develops. To do this I must *accept* my nervousness. I do not say, "Why can't I stop this horrible nervousness? I must get hold of myself!" Rather, I say, "I am nervous and I am going to be nervous and *that's all right!* In fact I am going to try to be *even more* nervous. In this way I may be able to find out *how* I make myself nervous by exaggerating how I do it. And while I do this, I am going to concentrate on my body and locate all the places where my nervousness manifests itself—where I *manifest myself to me!*" This will be painful and upsetting. But as I do this, I will start to come together. I will become aware of my inner self, and I can even have my nervous self and my controlling self have a conversation. I can talk to my nervousness, and my inner self can observe the encounter. This will be illustrated in more detail in a later chapter.

"But when I am worried about my child, my wife, my husband, how can I just let my worry go on? I need some kind of help to make me able to help them if I am needed."

Do you really feel your worrying helps anybody? And is it your child whom you really want to *help*—or do you resent him for allowing you to upset yourself? And do you really want to punish him? Only you can answer these questions. But you must answer them honestly, authentically. You can only do this if your worry and the real source and target of your worry come out. If your neighbor assuages, calms, mollifies you, the worry never fully comes out. And you can't see how you did it, how you worried yourself that way. This is just another case of the upsetting which we talked of in chapter 3. It needs to come out and be fully encountered. Then the two sides of the worry—perhaps the fear and resentment—can come together and be united.

"And now to depression. When everything seems to go wrong and the whole world is against me—what can I do then?"

We did a bit of this in chapter 4 in discussing the valleys of feeling. Valleys are a natural part of life and as such must be accepted—like worrying and nervousness. They cannot be filled up or cut off. They must just *be!* They will go. They will change if you give the cycle of life a chance to have its full swing. Can you afford to see your depression as something *you* did and not what *they* did to you? Can you accept it? Can you avoid the salve of your sympathetic friend? Can you accept her ear and reject the saccharine of her tongue? If so, fine! If not, perhaps you need another ear—one which will help you to be on your own, let you face yourself and come together with the mechanisms of your depression. Perhaps you need a person— or a way—to go with you into your depression and see how it—how you—work when you are depressed. If you can do this—if you can find this—you can learn to understand your depression as a natural phase of your life—anyone's life—just as necessary as your peaks of elation, particularly if you understand that peaks follow valleys. It is only as you learn to ride with this depression that you really get to know it and in the process get to know the many sides of your self.

We must now introduce another factor in the experiences of pain, discomfort, and control which has heretofore been neglected. That is the matter of diet. We all know that foods can be toxic or nourishing. If so, certain foods—the toxic ones—can lower bodily resistance and cause the body to suffer headaches, be the prey of disease bacteria, or cause gastronomic upset. These upsets need to be purged by "natural" means. Natural means would include eating nourishing, nontoxic foods and allowing the body to rest and heal itself. We shall hear more of this in chapter 8.

But foods can also affect emotional states as well. The energy level of the body, the blood sugar level, the metabolic level are all linked to endocrine functioning and hence to emotional states and emotional changes. My nervousness, worrying, depression, and peak experiences are all interwoven with what I eat and drink, as well as how I look at and feel about myself. It is a fabric of many strands and colors and all are necessary in order to make and maintain the whole.

Furthermore there are toxic people who can poison us in the same way toxic foods do. We need to recognize them, to purge ourselves of them if we have "ingested" them, and to avoid them, if at all possible, except in small unavoidable doses. These ideas about what is toxic and what is nourishing in both the gastronomic and the psychological areas of life will be discussed in chapter 8. It is clear here, however, that another avenue for dealing with my feelings, emotions and thoughts is through my diet.

So we see that losing control of emotions, pains, and discomfort means riding with them and accepting them as a necessary part of me—of my life. When I experience these supposed irritations as part of me, I get to know me and how I work. Often these emotions and bodily functions will be extreme. In these extreme phases, they can purge my body—me—of my toxic accumulations of material or psychic waste. These purges will help to unify me and heal me. They will bring me more fully together. I can also knit myself together through my choice of ideas, foods, and people. I can go *with* my headache and let the knowledge I gain there direct my life more effectively in what I eat and how I look at my self. I can accept toxic eliminations of all kinds in my life—physiological or psychological—as natural functions which, though painful, are necessary for my health, and try to understand them more fully. I can learn to accept my fevers—psychological and physiological—as part of my on-going organismic process. I can ride with my nervousness, worry, and depression and realize how delicately they are related to what I eat and how I think. In doing all this I am trying to see all sides of myself and to accept all sides. But better than that, I am trying to feel myself as one—as a whole. I am trying to get in touch with my inner, unifying self.

7

The
Tornado of Depression
And Its Escapes

"It is all very well to ride with feelings. But how would you like to guide your canoe into a whirlpool or fly your airplane into a tornado? Well, my depressions are just like that. They twist me, turn me, capture me, and then dash me against the rocks of despair. I am literally out of control, destroyed for hours, even days! I moan and object. But it has me in its power and I can't seem to get loose no matter how I try. Finally the storm runs its course, and I am free. Who knows when it will strike again?"

"My feeling of depression is like a giant straightjacket—a monster, a serpent—which has me in its grip. It arrives suddenly without warning. And it takes me over and paralyzes me. I can't move. I am entirely wrapped up in the torture of my depression. All the world and everything in it looks black. There is no hope. So I can only submit and suffer. I do not, and cannot, fight it. Eventually it gets tired and leaves as quickly as it arrived."

These are two views of deep depression and how it is perceived by one who is in its throes. While the first one seems more active and violent, both are equally devastating and incapacitating. The sufferer in each case has lost control and his only form of resistance—such as it is—is a verbal one, a protest against things as they are, against his fate, usually expressed in a passive form. Things are done *to* him. He is powerless, or feels that he is. He really can't do anything about it at all! He is caught up in this phenomenon as though it were a monster or a storm of some kind. He almost pleads to be free of the depression, but does not know by what means, or by what agent, he can be freed. Therefore his words are really addressed to no one.

At this point, were someone to offer him release from his torture, he would most certainly accept, if it could be administered to him by someone else, as for example, a pill, a drink, a hypodermic. Were the release effective, the "cure" would most certainly be repeated as was described with the aspirin in chapter 6. Were someone to suggest that he voluntarily go with his depression—go deeper—the sufferer would most certainly scoff at, or ignore, the suggestion and consider the offerer to be some unsympathetic person who had never known *his* kind of a depression.

However, going with this depression, as was described in the last chapter, is probably the only sure way to influence the course of the depression in a positive way. It may be the only way to shorten or mitigate the effect of the depression and in any sense to bring it under control. But it is so unreasonable—so painful, so ridiculous—that it is almost certain to be rejected. Let us turn from this dilemma, then, and look at some of the more usual ways in which we react to a tornado of depression.

> "When I am depressed, I am so down that I need a lift, and lift to me means a drink. When I am high—smashed—I feel strong. I can weather any storm, any depression, any misfortune. I am strong enough to attack and demolish anyone who wants to put me down and depress me. I feel free enough to unleash my hostilities toward them and I don't worry about the consequences."

What the speaker may be saying is:

> "When I am depressed, I feel with excruciating intensity. I cannot stand this pain. So I anesthetize myself, turn off my body. Then I can stand to go on. I feel strong because I have deadened myself·to the opposition which is within me. I have deadened my

controls and my sensitivities. From behind my alcoholic storm cellar, I need not be sensitive to whom I am attacking or how I do it. They are all shits! I just want to keep them off my back. And in attacking them, I am safe from being concerned with me."

Of course this technique only works temporarily—until the alcohol wears off. Then the depression is worse, and with it the liver and the kidneys. You deadened yourself to the opposition, but you did not deaden the opposition. All the while you were in your storm cellar, there were saboteurs working within. And though the effect of their demolition is delayed, it is very sure.

"When I get down, I eat. I feel weak and tired. I need nourishment, so I go to the refrigerator and really have a ball—cheese, cold cuts, ice cream, peanut butter—they will all do the trick. Leftover pie or cake is really great for energy. It doesn't really matter. What I really want is to be filled so that that tired, empty feeling is dissipated. Then I can go on, depression or not."

What he probably means is:

"I can't stand to be alone and my depressions are feelings of being alone—nobody cares. I don't really need food, but my emptiness seems to lie all in my stomach. As I fill me with food, I forget about others. And in filling myself—my stomach—my attention is drawn away from my other pains. I don't worry and wonder why I am alone."

This is all very well, but a stuffed stomach can't really take the place of friends. In a few hours, the bloat will take its effect and you will not only be alone, you will have serious indigestion, if not chronic gastric and intestinal problems. It is interesting that those who run to the gastronomic cavern to hide usually do it with the foods which are the most unhealthy. Hardly ever does such a person sit down to a good fresh salad or some lean rare meat.

"My depressions are very real and inescapable in my waking hours. When they hit, I get very fatigued and go to bed immediately. I have no trouble sleeping and can do it for hours when I have had a severe depression. I sometimes dream, but when I do it is at least a different scene. When I wake up it is a new day, and I have forgotten the intensity of my depression. It is gone."

This speaker probably means:

"I need to turn myself off when I am depressed, because I just don't know what to do. Nothing seems to work when I am awake, and furthermore I get so perplexed trying to handle it that I am afraid I will freak out. So I hit for my warm, soft bed, and soon I am in dreamland where I can handle things my way. I wish I could do it another way. I really don't need sleep. But what else can I do?"

Yes, you head for your womb where it feels soft and warm and safe. You solve no problems there, and if you have a dream you probably don't work with it as you might. Your lover, Morphus, God of sleep, is your solace. So you repeatedly run to his arms. It would be so nice if he would help you. But he can't take your problems away. They are not gone in the morning. They are just forgotten. They are bound to come back and are eventually apt to haunt your dreams as well. What can you do? What do you *want* to do! Keep your series of recurrent depressions, letting them get more intense and more confusing? Face your depression, in all its pain, and try to know yourself? Look for another turn off better than sleep? The choice is yours and yours alone!

"I have no real problems with intense depressions. Of course I have them, but I have a sure remedy. I just run to my lover, and in his arms—I mean in his bed—we fuck and forget. He is a beautiful lover. When I am with him, there is no room to worry or be upset. Thank God he is always available! I don't know what I would do if he ever left or got involved with someone else!"

If this speaker were more self-aware she might say:

My depressions really bug the hell out of me! I can't stand them and the intense pain they cause. So when they hit, I substitute the intense excitation of sex. I can turn on my organs of sexual arousal with my lover. and in this way I turn off my head and my other bodily pains. My lover is always ready for me because I am so turned on sexually at these times. I have no real confidence in him except as a sex machine. If he were more than this, I might get depressed with my relationship with him too! "

But, Miss Sexpot, do you see any future in this? Or do you even see any present? So you use your sexual arousal to anesthetize yourself to your pain. This pulls you apart. You become a sexual part and another part. The other part is wrestling with some kind of pain, worry, upset. And you can't take it. You can't take yourself—your *total* self. So you use one part of your self against another. And the battle goes on inside, but one side is deluged temporarily by the compulsive force and violence of the other. You drown part of you in the surge of sex. What happens after sex is over, or in between sex exploits? Or must you be committed to a life of continual, compulsive sex in order to drown your worrying self?

We have listed some of the escapes from the tornado of depression when it sweeps in on us, unannounced and unwanted. But is it really unannounced? Perhaps there are "straws in the wind" that show what is in store. Perhaps a long, still, seemingly calm spell in my life may be a time when "static charge" is accumulating. Perhaps this is a time when emotional buildup is growing gradually due to a lack of opportunity for adequate release. Perhaps full sexual release is lacking. Perhaps work and living are so productive and successful that the only sparks are those from my nose against the grindstone. Perhaps I am squelching minor irritations unconsciously in the attempt to save face or keep the peace. Any or all of these may be taking place and as they grow, little by little, the scene is set for the tornado.

And is it unwanted? A tornado is something dramatic and powerful. At least it is never boring no matter how destructive it is. It does clear lots of accumulated debris and results in a lot of new building from the ground up. And, finally, what would we do without the necessary "electric" release of the emotional discharge of the tornado? The lack of this discharge might cause a much more destructive effect internally—an ulcer or a coronary.

However—back to our original question—what to do about a tornado? How do we live with it?

First, let's agree that the escapes—all those listed above and many others—are more destructive in the long run than the tornado could ever be. We have described these destructive effects in detail above.

Second, if we are to live with it, and we can't squelch it, we had better understand it. We need to see that a tornado of depression does grow

65

gradually, even though its development is "invisible" to those close at hand. We must also realize that since it is so violent, its life is short—in fact it is self-terminating. If we can only suffer a bit, it will be over in a relatively painless fashion—more painless than all the supposedly helpful escapes or cures.

Third, a tornado of depression does have a few beneficial effects. It clears away lots of emotional rubbish and archaic emotional structures. It allows, even requires, us to reconstruct in a fundamental way.

Finally, and perhaps most important, a tornado of depression allows us to know ourselves in a very penetrating way. If we will stay *with* it, *in* it, feel its force and feel the pain it produces as it rages through us and against us, we get to know the depths of our being. We know how we operate, where we are weak, and where we are strong.

To stay with the tornado takes real guts. It also takes the willingness to describe and express exactly how the depression affects us; how we treat ourselves during it; and how we react to other people, other things, and other forces in our lives. To stay with the tornado also takes real practice with the skills and techniques of staying with it, *before* it ever hits. We need to learn how to stay in there without escaping or squelching it. The skills of doing this will be described in more detail in a later chapter.

8

Poison

vs.

Nourishment

What is the Difference?

"I really enjoyed that meal! When I got up from the table I could hardly move. I had second and third helpings of everything, even the apple pie a la mode. My only regret is that I couldn't hold more. Don't know when I've had such a satisfying experience! Wish I could have a dinner like that every night!"

"They hardly fed me anything—a little thin soup, a tossed green salad with very little dressing, and some undercooked, tasteless meat. No dessert! No hot bread! No nothing! I was starved. When we were finished, my ribs were really sticking together. After I left, I had to stop and get a hamburger and some french fries to fill me up. Then I felt better!"

"When I get off the train, its only a short walk home—about six blocks. On cold nights, I usually stop in at the Casa Blanca and have a few martinis before going on. That way I am not so tired and on edge when I get home and I can "face the music" better. Then, too, I like the guys who hang out there at that time. They're all friendly and seem to want to share all the news they have heard during the day—who's doing what with whom, etc. They have lots of jokes, lots of laughs. I really feel good with them. I'm only sorry I can't stay longer."

"Tom is a really good friend of mine. Whenever we meet, he has loads of questions to ask me and things to tell me. He seems to get into all kinds of problems and flatters me by thinking I can solve them all. Of course, I don't mind listening. And I do feel he needs my ear, poor fellow! Don't know whom he would turn to if it weren't for me! When I leave him, sometimes I really feel beat—glad I can get home to another scene. But I'm always ready to help. And he knows it!"

"When I was lost on that mountain, I was panicky! I didn't know where I was or where to go! I tried to climb up higher to see further, but all my surroundings confused me. I had no food. I had no companions. My friends had gone on while I explored the cave. And when I came out, it was getting late. No time to look further. My impulse was to shout. Only silence answered me. In desperation, I went back to the cave, realizing I would have to spend the night there alone. I went in a short way to escape the cold and exposure outside. I was dreadfully hungry. I did not even have a green twig to chew on. I leaned up against what seemed to be the most comfortable spot and tried to rest and relax. This I did for awhile because I was very tired. But my thoughts of home and of my companions kept creeping in to worry me. Also, how was I every going to find my way back? Finally I slept. It was a cold night, but in the morning the rising sun reached into the cave and woke me. I felt hungry and stiff and sore. But in the morning light the trail was now clearly visible to me. That breakfast I ate when I got back to our camp is the best I can ever remember!"

"Yes, Cindy is a wonderful wife. We have an exciting life together, but it is anything but calm and smooth. She has her ways of keeping and not keeping the house. And I have my little demands. Often she understands. But on occasion she can't take it (take me and my demands) and she sings out loud and clear. Of course I don't keep silent either. On such nights the middle of our bed is a cold, vacant valley. But by the dawn's early light, things look much better to both of us. We don't apologize, we rarely recriminate. We just go on and take each other's rough edges as they are. I once thought we would fit smoothly together. Now I know it can't happen—*no way!*

The six individuals who are talking above are telling us about people and food and their feelings and reactions to them. Sometimes they seem to be satisfied. Sometimes not. Sometimes their reactions are mixed or not too clear. Although people and food affect us in many ways, let us attempt to concentrate on whether the food and persons described above are poisonous or *toxic* to the speakers, or whether they are *nourishing*. It may help if we first answer the questions, "When is something toxic? When is it nourishing?"

A toxic food is a food which really is not a food at all. It does not supply anything which is necessary for life. In fact most toxic things are really death-producing rather than life-sustaining. Too much of them will cause death. A nourishing food is one which gives to the body something which is life-sustaining and life-producing It makes the body more alive, more full of life, after it is eaten.

It is obvious that not all "foods" are nourishing. We can only tell whether a food is nourishing or toxic by the effect it has on the body. And sometimes the toxicity does not show up immediately. We can, then, not afford to judge a food by its appearance, its taste, or even its label. Fortunately, there are enough studies on diet and nutrition to guide the careful person in his search for nourishing foods and to help him to avoid toxic ones. Unfortunately these studies are all too few and poorly publicized. Also there are many food fads, advertisements, and sources of misinformation from supposed experts which make it easy for us to be confused and misled.

To answer specifically our two questions in regard to food, let us say that a food is toxic when it interferes with the life-sustaining processes of the body or when it does not supply the body with any life-sustaining material. A food is nourishing when it aids and supports the life-sustaining processes or when it supplies material to the body which is life-sustaining.

Now let us talk about toxic and nourishing people. In doing this I shall be drawing from the works of Dr. Jerry Greenwald who first used these terms to describe types of persons.

A toxic person lacks the ability to initiate activities that will nourish him. He continually seeks and calls on others to nourish him, and he doubts his ability to stand on his own two feet and be autonomous. Insofar as he is toxic, he is really a nonperson—a non-individual—as he cannot deal with himself or assert himself for himself. When he is alone he is miserable, so he continually seeks others who will nourish him. When he finds such a person he will demand or plead for nourishment. In his desire to suck or pull nourishment from this other, he tends to destroy the relationship and must then go on to another. This means that his relationships are often short-lived. When he does form a more lasting relationship, it almost always results in the other person being sucked dry. If this happens, the other person becomes toxic too. His nourishment and ability to nourish are destroyed, and they must both seek other relationships as they can not long stand each other's toxicity.

One of the tragedies of the toxic person is that he is so other-oriented that he never really takes a good look at himself or gets to know himself. Therefore he does not know what capacities he has for self-nourishment and automatically feels that he is lacking in ability and self-worth. It is for this reason that he is other-oriented. He is other-oriented because he feels he is worthless, and he feels he is worthless because of his other-orientation. This vicious circle traps him continually and defeats the plans of most other people to help him. He is, of course, unaware of his pernicious effect on others and interprets their rejection of his attempts to suck them dry as a confirmation of his opinion of his own worthlessness. When the other person attempts to nourish him, he only sucks all the harder. Should the other person attempt to help him be attentive to what he is doing, the message will fall on deaf ears or be interpreted as a personal rejection or a put-down. Therefore, the humanitarian other is likely to be toxified himself, rejected by the toxic person, or find it necessary, after prolonged contact with the toxic person, to, himself, get a richer source of nourishment due to his own badly depleted reservoirs. In this way it is possible for a toxic person to so spread the "disease" that a whole group or community of "kind" and "helpful" persons may be toxified. Their only escape, other than personal rejection and scapegoating, is to insist on being realistic with the toxic one, calling his attention to what he is doing and rejecting his over-demands for nourishment. This means that nourishment would be given in accordance with the desire of the giver, not in response to the demands of the toxic one. Over-demands would be rejected, but nourishment would still flow. In this way the spread of toxicity might be reduced. But it is important to realize in doing this that a strong "No!" must be said, and that this "No!" will be painful to the toxic one. Any attempt to continually avoid pain will mean to say "Yes!" to the toxic one, and to say "Yes!" continually is to spread toxicity and be toxified in the process.

A nourishing person is a self-sustaining person, insofar as he is nourishing. He can and does supply his own nourishment. He enjoys being alone, but also enjoys the company of others. When he is alone, he has many ways of nourishing himself and taking care of himself. He has a desire to know himself and is continually seeking ways to further this knowledge. He often communes with his deeper feelings when alone and develops a self-richness by doing this.

When he is with other people, the nourishing person seeks to know them better and is stimulated by their contact. He does not demand knowledge from them but lets it flow according to the other person's desires. He enjoys himself, so he enjoys sharing his feelings and experiences with others. However, he does not push himself on others and is sensitive to the way others react to his behavior. In this way his contacts with others also further his self-knowledge. He is always learning about himself and his abilities, and in these ways is learning to be able to nourish himself even better.

In contrast to the toxic person, the nourishing person does not seek to control others or his relationship with them. He wants other people to be themselves. In this way he can more truly know them in an authentic manner. Should the other person reject some plan or idea of his, this is OK. And he will be just as free to say his own "No!" not meaning at all a necessary rejection of the person. What he does not want or feels negative toward, he rejects. What he does desire and feels positive toward, he accepts and moves toward. He feels no strong desire to suck or pull from others, for he has plenty of nourishment in himself. However, he readily accepts what is given or offered by another whenever it appeals to him. And he is glad to give to others things which he values and wants to give. He would not be unduly hurt if, on occasion, his gifts were not acceptable to someone else.

We cannot always tell a toxic person from a nourishing person at first acquaintance. In fact, it may take a somewhat lengthy contact with a person before we can evaluate his effect. This is similar to the effect of foods—the taste is not enough. Furthermore the "label" (or reputation) of the person is not enough to identify him either. A person may be toxic to one person and not to another. For example, a mother, in her over-concern and over-demands, may be toxic to her son. In her relation to her adult friends, she may be very nourishing, demanding nothing and accepting her friends as they are. Also, many people mistake an overly outgoing toxic person for a nourishing one, if they have not had a chance to look into his effect on themselves deeply enough. It is a human tragedy that foods and persons are often falsely packaged and erroneously advertised, either out of ignorance or the attempt to deceive for some supposed greater profit. This means that we should avoid categorizing a person as T (toxic) or N (nourishing) too quickly. We need to experience him fully. Then the effect on us will dictate how we should react to him.

We should be aware that, in contrast to foods, no person is purely T or N. We have some characteristics—some styles of behavior—that are T and some that are N. If we are aware of ourselves, we can see this and correct it as we wish. We can become more nourishing, by strengthening our sources for self-sufficiency and self-knowledge. And we can become less toxic by eliminating our needs to control, to suck from others, and to be overly dependent on them. However, it is also possible to become less nourishing and more toxic. This will usually be an unconscious development, due to a blindness resulting from some form of trauma, tension, or shock. It is almost inevitable that blocks to self-knowledge result in an increase in toxicity. For as the individual becomes out of touch with himself, he is likely to split and work against himself. As he does this, he will become insecure and seek dependence, support, and nourishment from others. If the split grows, the hanging on to others will increase and, with it, the toxicity. If this happens, a person's whole behavior may be permeated with toxicity. On the other hand we can develop our self-knowledge, our togetherness, and our wholeness to the point where we are very solid, secure, and able to nourish ourselves in most of our patterns of behavior. In this case we may be characterized as predominantly N.

It seems probable that many persons grow to be predominately T or

N once they pass a balance point in their personal development. After a certain amount of self-knowledge, a lasting desire will have developed to get more and more of it and so become more N. After a certain amount of dependence is built up, the vicious circle develops—the lack of self-knowledge causes the lack of self-worth causes the lack of self-knowledge—and the person becomes more and more T. Many of us may never reach either of these balance points and may exist all of our lives with a relatively even balance between T and N in our patterns of behavior. Those who know us in one area of life may then relate to us as T. Those who relate to us in another area may relate to us as N. In reality we are predominantly neither, and these partial judgments tend to keep us where we are and prevent us from moving past the balance point in either direction.

Now back to our two original questions, "When is something toxic? When is it nourishing?" A person is toxic when he drains my sustenance past my desire to give, when he tries to control me in my relations with him and demands responses from me which are not authentic, and when he refuses to be responsible, self-sufficient, or self-aware.

A person is nourishing when he can and does give nourishment to others, when he can and does receive nourishment from others, and particularly when he can and does responsibly nourish himself. To do this he must be self-aware and sensitive to others as well.

Nourishing people give and receive that which is life-sustaining and build their individuality and wholeness as well as the individuality and wholeness of others. Nourishing foods do the same for the body. Toxic people drain sustenance and interfere with the development of the wholesome integrity of the person. Toxic foods do the same.

What can one do about that which is toxic except to avoid it? How can one develop a higher degree of nourishing power? What can I do if I have ingested toxic food for most of my life? What can I do if I am associated with toxic people in most of my life activities?

The answers are clear here, but not easy. If my stomach is full of poison, I must vomit. If my life is surrounded by a circle of poisonous people, I must regurgitate them too! As objectionable as both of these acts are, they are the only effective first step. I would not expect to live with an overdose of sleeping tablets in my stomach. I cannot live, really, surrounded by a circle of "friends" who suck me dry. I must *by force* reject both of these situations. This is a necessity in order to survive!

But suppose it is not my stomach? Suppose my tissues, my organs, my blood have been toxified? Or suppose my home, my work, and all my associations are permeated with toxic people? Then vomiting won't do it. My body—or my life—must be treated with health-giving food or health-giving associations. I must be aware of and choose good food after I have decided which foods I ate were toxic. And I must be aware of the toxic associations and gradually substitute nourishing ones for toxic ones. However, in each case the first step is to *stop* the toxicity! *Stop* eating the toxic food! *Stop* associating with the toxic people! It will probably be necessary for me to fast for a while to get over the toxicity and let myself—my body—get back to a healthy normal condition. In each case, a poisoned body or a poisoned psyche can well stand a little starving in order to get back together with itself and take a healthy look at things. Then—and only then—can I carefully begin to eat. Then and only then can I carefully begin to associate in nourishing ways with nourishing foods and people.

But what does it mean to fast? When I have an upset stomach, do I not need to "doctor it," to put something in it to "cure" it? When I have had an unfortunate love affair, do I not need to find someone else quickly—almost anyone—who will treat me right? The answer to these questions is not always clear, for individual cases may differ. However, toxicity in gastronomic or psychological affairs is damaging and destructive. It usually needs a time of healing. During this period, the body (or the person) collects its forces, licks its wounds as it were, and attempts to take stock of the situation. This is a time of self-nutrition, of getting to know one's self, of feeling one's body, and plumbing the depths of one's anguish. After several weeks of this experience "in the wilderness," perhaps we are better able to go on to our major decisions. Were we not to fast, we would probably go on and commit the same painful self-tortures to which we subjected ourselves before. Hence, the repeated unsuccessful marriages in rapid succession. Hence, the repeated unsuccessful reducing diets. We insist on a cure—any cure—but it must be rapid, even though the disease—the unsuccessful marriage—took years to generate.

But what about the six people we started with? Where do they come in? Are they toxic or nourishing? Are their desires for food and people healthy or not? Let us take a more careful look at them now.

The speaker in the first two anecdotes might have been the same man. He certainly likes full, rich, satisfying meals and he can't stand thin, tasteless ones. If asked whether he likes to be nourished, he would undoubtedly answer with a resounding, "Yes!" But does he, perhaps, confuse satisfaction with nourishment? Could he, perhaps, be used to having more to eat than is nourishing for him? Is it possible that his desire for sweets and starches is not healthful? In that case might his idea of gastronomic satisfaction really be toxic for him? In order for him to answer these questions he would have to investigate further than his immediate taste and bodily feelings and try to see what were the longer range results of his patterns of eating. He would need to see, in the long run, whether or not what he eats contributes to his overall bodily health—whether it is essentially life-sustaining.

In the third anecdote the speaker seems to need a lift which he seeks through martinis and light conversation. He feels so good in this setting that he regrets leaving. Could one, with any legitimacy, question whether his lift were more nearly an escape? Do his activities at the Casa Blanca merely help him to put off going home? Is he more able, really, to "face the music" when he does get home? Is the alcohol toxic or nourishing to him? Does it supply him with life-sustaining value? And are his friends at the Casa Blanca helping him to nourish himself? Or is he developing a toxic dependence on them? To answer these questions we would have to observe the third speaker's behavior and study his body processes and bodily condition more thoroughly.

In the fourth anecdote, Tom certainly needs a friend. But what kind of a friend does he need? Does he need one to milk dry, one whom he can exhaust? Or does he need a friend who will level with him and give a bit more than an ear? And is the speaker really a good friend? We could only answer this by observing their behavior together more carefully and by talking to Tom as well. Then we could see to what extent this relationship was toxic or nourishing.

In the fifth anecdote we see a person who is alone and in distress. He is on his own with no resources at hand. Does he seem to be able to sustain and nourish himself at all times? If not, are there any times when he does sustain himself? Are there times when he does not? On the basis of these answers, would you consider this person predominantly toxic or nourishing?

The sixth anecdote shows clearly a marital relationship which is not always smooth. Yet the speaker describes Cindy as "a wonderful wife." Would their relationship be more nourishing if they agreed with each other more? Is each one helping the other to sustain himself more effectively? Or are they developing an undue independence from each other so that they will have to seek out a third person to nourish them? If we could observe them, we might be able to tell. In any event *they* could answer these questions if they would take stock of their relationship from time to time.

We see, now, that food and people must be carefully chosen if we want life to be sustained. In choosing, mistakes in both areas are bound to occur. What appears on first contact to be nourishing, may turn out to be toxic. The crucial need then, is the ability and strength to say "No!" to the toxic both before and after the choice. Excluding the toxic is hard, but rejecting the toxic after it is chosen is even harder and more painful. It is because of this pain that healing is so necessary after the toxic food or person has been rejected. To initiate the process of healing, a fast is usually very desirable if not absolutely necessary. In the next chapter we shall see how touch can play a role in healing as well as in nourishing in general.

9

The Magic
of
Touch

Touch is magic. It is mysterious because it is so powerful and so important, yet so insignificant. It is symbolic, and yet it can be a sign of nothing at all. Touch is ecstatically delightful, and yet can cause excruciating pain. It is known throughout the living universe. It is a necessity for life itself. Yet it is by touch that we kill and cause "the kiss of death." Touch is never forgotten. It is always remembered in the body. And yet it happens in the present. Touch only happens now!

There are also many kinds of touches. There is the touch of the hand as an introduction; it says, "This is me. I am open to you!" There is the touch of control; it announces, "I am afraid of you as you are. I want to control you, change you!" There is the touch of fear which pleads, "I am quivering, cold, alone. Protect me! Shelter me!" There is the touch of comfort; it says, "I feel with you and want you to know I am here." There is the touch of love; it whispers, "I am resonating, vibrating with you! I want you now and tomorrow!" There is the touch of resentment and punishment; it snarls, "I hate you. I want to punish you and make you feel my anger!" There is the touch of rejection; it says, "Get away! Get out of my way! Don't interfere!" And there are, of course, many other varieties of touch too numerous to mention here. Among these are the touches of which I am not aware and the strictly internal touching which goes on within my body. These were already discussed in chapter 2.

In this chapter, we are concerned with the touches where at least one agent is external and where there is an awareness of what is happening in the situation. It is in these touches that the magic is most powerful.

"But what is the magic of touch? Isn't touch just friction of skin against skin, or sound against eardrum, or light within the eye? I love a massage, or a beautiful painting, or the beautiful sounds of music, but why the big deal about it?"

Perhaps it might help if we listen to a few persons talk about touch. We will have to listen carefully to what they say. It would be better if we could listen to the tone of their voices, for they will be speaking to us on many levels, and the messages often become confused.

"When I first met him, he did not shake my hand or touch me. He just looked me straight in my eyes and repeated my name. I felt as though he were looking into my soul and body, that he could feel the increased beat of my heart and the depth of my breathing, that he could somehow know the vibration that was going on through my arms and legs. We sat down and tried to converse about inconsequential things—work, school, politics, weather, even our mutual contacts with our host of the evening. This was a necessary stream of interaction on which our mutual involvement impressed its patterns. Our words were largely meaningless. But the tone of our voices, and our facial expressions spoke eloquently. As he spoke, I responded—sometimes only by a look or gesture. And when I spoke, I could feel the responding chord come from him.

"So it went on until the phone call. When he returned, it was as though a curtain had been dropped between us. He was way out there. And my words developed the hollow sound of an echo. His eyes were glassy, mine were questioning, anxious, and finally resentful. I reached out for his hand, but it was cold and lifeless. I excused myself and left. It was over, at least for now. We had touched deeply, perhaps too deeply for him. I could not stand the empty coldness after the glowing warmth before."

"As she came toward me, I could see that something was wrong. She glared at me and her eyes shot sparks throughout the room. I was upset and a bit curious. What was it now? Soon I found out though she never mentioned her by name. Did she really suspect *me*? How ridiculous! I had hardly touched her, even if I did *look* at her very attentively at dinner. It made me burn! And I shot my sparks back. I would give her as good as she gave!

"When we got up to leave, I took her coat to hold it for her. She begrudgingly let me, and I responded with my own controlling grip on her shoulders after the coat was on. She turned around and glared at me and we proceeded with our not-so-smiling good nights and polite thank you's for 'a most enjoyable evening and a delightful dinner.' She beat me to the car and stood shivering at the door as I unlocked it for her. On the way home we were miles apart on the narrow front seat. The fan of the car heater whirred warmly, but our mutual coldness was too much for it. I knew it would be a long, cold night and I was thankful for the new dual-control electric blanket on our bed."

Let us look at what these two couples are saying to each other, and also at what they indirectly tell us about touch. The first couple is enthralled with each other without any physical touch at all. They respond to each other by words, by look, by gesture. Each and every one of these messages was touching. It produced a *bodily* reaction even though there was no direct bodily contact. These "touches" were reciprocal. As a charge of feeling flowed from one person to the other, a reinforcing charge of feeling was returned by the other person. So the feeling continued to rise. They were, at this point, nourishing each other as far as feelings were concerned. Then the phone call. Here "death" occurred—the death of the rising feeling. He was emptied of nutriment, nor could he take any. He was toxified and could not function at all except as a poisoner. His partner tried, but could not penetrate the toxicity. Now the feelings were still reciprocal but not reinforcing. He responded to her approach by blank coldness. This caused her response to progressively change from nourishing to toxic. Very wisely she left the scene and refused to be toxified.

The second couple is experiencing a different tone of emotion. She is resentful and her resentment is responded to in kind by her escort. He becomes even more resentful. The depth of this emotion grows reciprocally throughout the evening until they depart. Then a coldness sets in. There is no nourishing going on. But there evidently has not been any nourishing going on at all throughout the evening. From the beginning they were poisoning each other by playing at controlling each other and attempting to squelch each other's individuality. After they left the party, they pull apart. They are not nourishing each other now. Nor are they poisoning each other. They seem to be fasting—perhaps healing. If there is any nourishing possible, perhaps it can go on in the morning.

These couples tell us, furthermore, that although touch need not be directly physical, it is a thing of the body. When I am touched, I am touched *in my body*. I know it because I *feel* it, and I can—if I care to do so—locate it in my body. Touch is also reciprocal. When I *send* out a message of love, control, fear, resentment, or openness, I also *receive* a message in return. It may be a reinforcing message: My look of interest may receive a responding look of interest. Or my look of interest may receive a responding message of disinterest. In this case my message is diminished by the response. Nevertheless to touch means to be touched by another. To every touch there is a responding touch. Even a blank wall, if I touch it, gives me a response, although it may be a cold, blank one. This is the real magic of touch. Whenever I reach out—by word, hand, look, or gesture—if my reaching is clear and direct, I will not only produce a feeling in another, but I will also produce a feeling in myself. We must now add a footnote to our title: "I can only touch you now. But when I do, I also touch me now." Touching, therefore, is a mutual experience whether it be constructive or destructive. It is imperative and it is now.

This raises the questions, "How do I want to touch you? And how do I want to be touched?" As we saw in chapter 8, we all want to be nourished. But if you respond to my "nourishing touch" with resentment, or toxicity of any other kind, what do I do? I have many choices. I can continue to attempt to touch you in a "nourishing" manner, hoping to dilute, overcome, or neutralize what I perceive as your toxic response. For example, suppose you are tired, upset, or suffering from indigestion. I can try to minister to you by inquiring about your upset or fatigue, or by trying to get food or medicine for you. I can do this repeatedly, hoping to get you out of this condition. However you may not know the real nature of your condition. You cannot explain it. You only want to be left alone. My attempt to deluge you with supposed nutriment is seen by you as highly toxic. Actually it may be that I cannot stand you when you are upset, and I am unconsciously trying to control you by this attempt at pseudonourishing. Therefore you respond, quite naturally, with resentment to my deluge and your response is quite in tune with what may be the underlying motive for my supposedly nourishing touches. I see you, however, as unreasonably toxic in your response. If I were to get in touch with my own feelings and behavior, I might see what I am doing. In any event, it is questionable whether a toxic response can ever be overpowered or deluged by a nourishing one. When I see what I. am doing, I had better pull back and let you heal yourself. If I don't do this, my repeatedly repulsed attempts at "nourishing" you are very likely to turn to mutual resentment, mutual toxification. If I want to give and receive nourishment, I had better first be clear whether I am *really* giving it or not. Your responses are a very good clue to this. If our responses turn out to be mutually toxic there is nothing to be gained by continuing. At such times a fast and a healing period are in order.

But suppose my touches are nourishing and you enjoy them and feed on them—then do we have it made? Not necessarily. I can still overfeed you if I am not careful. Can I stand to be told that you have had enough? Or do I have to continue, since I see myself in no other role than your nourisher? It is hoped that I know when to stop, and that I can also stand to receive nourishment from you. I must be able to stand care, concern, and feeding from you—and respond to this in a nontoxic way.

Also I am nourished when I touch you in a nourishing fashion. My body feels good, my words feel good, my looks at you feel good when they nourish you, when they reinforce, support, and complement you. But I must nurse at your breasts too. I must glow at your words, your touches, your food of all kinds and so let you be touched in this reciprocal fashion! If we do these things in a creative noncontrolling way, and if we can stand a few dry breezes of toxicity, on occasion, without coming apart, then the relationship has a good chance to be viable. This would be our message to the two couples who gave us the benefit of their feelings earlier.

Let us now look at the more physical aspects of touch, and also what it means to heal some one of toxicity. We have said repeatedly in discussing awareness, upsetting one's self, and depression that pervasive negative emotions are due to a split in the person. Sometimes this may be a split between mind and body, a split between a good and bad self, or a split between a topdog and an underdog. Whatever the nature of the split, the result is that the person is out of touch with himself and with the surrounding world. He is not together. Hence his perceptions of himself and the world are distorted. The basic split is in the body itself since the body is the physical analog of the personality. Any split in the person has a corresponding split in the body. Furthermore, it is with the body and its various organs of sensory awareness that we perceive the surrounding world. A distorted, split body cannot be in touch with itself or its surroundings.

What has been said of pervasive negative emotions is also true of toxicity. The toxic person does not know himself; he can not and does not look at himself. Due to a split body and a split mind, he does not perceive himself or his surroundings realistically. This is the reason why he relates so ineffectively with other people. This is the reason why he sucks them dry. He fears losing them because he doesn't know them. And he doesn't know them because of his split.

To heal toxicity or pervasive negative emotions means, then, to mend the split and to make the body and the person whole. It is interesting to note that the root meaning of "heal" and "whole" are the same and that "holy" comes from this same root also. Evidently to be holy—to be in the service of one's God, however that may be interpreted—means to be one, to be whole and together. In this condition, one is also *healed* and *healthy* and capable of functioning to the maximum extent of his capabilities. In this condition one is in touch with his inner self.

With this idea of holiness in mind, it is easy to see why many religions have emphasized the "laying on of hands" as a way of healing the sick and also as a part of the service of ordination of the priesthood in the service of God. It would seem that touch by the hands symbolically represents healing and making holy too. It also is used in the marriage ceremony to make the two able to live *together* as *one*—to make the couple a whole.

But is this laying on of hands more than symbolic? Like most religious symbols, one would suspect that originally the laying on of hands was a practice which had much more of a direct practical value than it is considered to have today. Hands were laid on actively, strongly, and skillfully so as to treat the bodies of those who needed healing of any kind. This would be true of those who needed to be particularly healthy for God's service as well as those who were actually sick. Then, too, the best way to learn how to heal would be to be made holy. And most early "priests" were first of all healers, casters-out of demons and sicknesses from the body.

Today this physical aspect of touch is again proving itself. Massage, in all of its aspects, is no longer just a luxury for the rich. In the opinion of many psychologists, it is becoming recognized as a necessity for us all. Studies of experimental rats seem to show that when deprived of touch they develop marasmus—a disease of malnutrition of the tissues—and eventually die. Other studies present evidence that children in overcrowded orphanages who are not handled frequently have a higher death rate. If our tissues are to be properly nourished, blood must flow to them. If blood is to flow, muscles and connecting tissues must be flexible, supple, and lithe, with no constricting blocks or knots. If muscles are to be lithe and supple, sensory energy must be able to flow freely and smoothly throughout the body so as to control, unify, and make whole (holy) this body. In this condition the body can better resist disease, put off the advance of old age, and use the energy available to it more efficiently for God's service (or whatever is the purpose of one's life).

But how are muscles, nerves, blood vessels and all the other tissues and organs of the body to achieve this condition? How is the body to be made whole?

First, the body must be fed the proper health-giving foods. This is the matter for another book and has already been excellently treated by Dr. Henry Bieler in *Food is Your Best Medicine*. Second is the "laying on of hands," the manipulation of the body so as to stimulate the tissues, improve blood circulation, increase the metabolic rate, and renew the flow of sensory energy throughout the body. This is being done by the followers of Dr. Ida Rolf in a technique called structural integration and is described very interestingly in "The Bulletin of Structural Integration." It is also being accomplished in a different way by the practitioners of bioenergetics, Dr. Alexander Lowen and his followers. This technique is described in *The Betrayal of the Body* by Lowen and also in *Pleasure* by the same author. There are, of course, many others who are skilled in the art of laying on hands, far too numerous to mention here. For the purposes of the present reader, let us describe some ways in which the magic of physical touch may be implemented.

The key idea in touching (for whatever purpose) is attentiveness. Both parties to the touch must be attentive to what is being experienced. As a preliminary exercise to the actual physical touching, a fantasy might be used. One person conducts the fantasy— a mini-vacation it might be called. He describes clearly and specifically a trip—to the beach. the mountains, to a forest for example. In describing the trip all details are given in the present and the other. person, or persons, follow in their imaginations. Sensory details are emphasized—the smell of salt spray, pine needles, flowers; the colors of sky, clouds, ocean, trees; the sound of wind, oceans, animals, rain; the touch of sand and leaves underfoot, or wind against the face or in the hair. The sequence of events is not important and is only necessary to give a flow to the fantasy. The trip should be conducted in the most relaxed condition possible. Eyes should be closed and illumination should be at a minimum. Sometimes a soft musical background helps.

When the trip is over, each person shares his bodily feelings and reactions to the trip. He is asked to do this in as great detail as possible so as to heighten the sensory reaction. Care should be taken to locate, as exactly as possible, where in the body the feeling was and how, if at all, it changed. In this way the body is turned on to touch in a distant and nonphysical way.

A second nonphysical touch activity is a sensory survey. Each person is asked to concentrate on the feeling in various parts of his body, starting at the top of his head and covering, in detail, all important body parts—these might include head and scalp, cheeks, eyes, lips, tongue and teeth, neck and chest, heart, stomach, belly, groin and genitals, arms, legs, shoulders, hips, hands, fingers, feet, toes, vertebrae and ribs. The sequence should be gradually covered and the path should be from one body part to another one close at hand. Large jumps should be eliminated so that the flow of sensory energy may be encouraged. As a result of these two exercises, the participants may learn to be attentive to sensory phenomena in various parts of their bodies. They may also learn that there are certain parts of their bodies where sensation is virtually dead.

In touching the body *physically* several cautions should be observed. Many persons are not used to being touched. Others have been told to avoid touching for a variety of reasons. These persons may take a very negative or fearful view of it. Even after the two preliminary exercises, touching some persons must be approached with caution.

The best place to start is with the hands. Shaking hands, one hand at a time, then with both hands, then holding further up on the forearms. Attention should be focused on what is being experienced, what is felt, and these feelings should be described and shared.

Next each person may spend five minutes on his partner's right hand alone, touching it all over with the toucher's two hands while the one being touched closes his eyes to heighten attentiveness to the feeling. The same may be done with the other hand and this followed by the touching of each foot.

Next a face get-to-know might follow. Here one person shuts his eyes while his partner touches each part of his face and head. The progress is slow and unhurried and should take more than five minutes. This exercise brings more intimacy and more variable sensations.

After these exercises, we are probably ready for touching of the trunk of the body as well as legs and arms. There are two ways of introducing' this. One is by finger-tip touch in imitation of raindrops. This starts on top of the head and proceeds slowly to cover neck, shoulders, arms, back, shoulders and gradually back up to the head.

The other exercise is a slapping exercise which is concentrated on neck, shoulders, arms, back, and legs. It should move from head to feet and back again and is best done when the subject is lying face down on the floor.

This may be followed by pressing with both hands, first on the shoulders, then in the middle of the back and finally in the small of the back. The pressure should be light and last about thirty seconds in each position with a period of twenty seconds in between pressing when there is no touch at all. After each of these exercises, subjects should be asked to share feelings and should be encouraged to describe their feelings and emotions in intimate detail. Were it possible, these exercises should lead to a complete massage and stroking of the whole body, excepting the genitals and erogenous zones. However, this requires great skill and also is not usually acceptable to most persons as it goes far beyond their threshold of modesty. All of these exercises should be carried out by partners who take turns being toucher and being touched.

These are only a few of the kinds of touching exercises which are available and which are now being used in many centers of growth and personal development. In describing them, I have drawn heavily from the work of William Schutz in his book *Joy* and from Bernard Gunther in his *Sense Relaxation*. There are many sources describing other techniques, but they are now far too numerous to include here.

We have seen, then that touch is magical in that it is always a two-way effect. When I touch you, I touch me too! We have seen that touch is always now and is inherently of the body. We have looked at the nonphysical ways of touching and described some exercises for developing ways to heighten sensory awareness by touch, both physical and nonphysical. We have also seen that touch is not a luxury but is now, and always was, a necessity for life. It is enough to conclude with Michelangelo's idea that God created man by touch. Did man in this process also touch God?

10

The Encounter

As a Way

of

Riding with Feelings

Under*: Why do you hold me back? Why won't you let me give? Why do you tie me up every time I get close to expressing myself fully? I feel so uptight I could scream! But you won't even let me do that! The sounds sticks in my throat. All I feel is the terrible tightness in my throat, the tension in my shoulders, the knot in my stomach! You are almost incapacitating me! Why do you do these things to me?

Top*: Because that way I have you under control. You won't get out of hand and get into something you can't handle! That way you are safe! And you like it that way too!

Under: I do not! I want out! I want to free, loose, expressive! I want to let myself go! I want to kick you out—get rid of you for good!

Top: Oh, do you? Well just kick me out then if you dare. But I won't go! I know what is best for you. So I'm staying right here. Just listen to your voice. It's no louder than a whisper. My voice is much stronger! If you want me to go, you've got to sound like you *mean* it!

*If these terms are confusing, see page 98 for an explanation of what they mean.

Under: BUT I DO MEAN IT! DO YOU HEAR THAT! I HATE YOU! I HATE YOU! GET OUT! GET OUT! GET OUT! (Sobs convulsively.) I wish I could get free and be open and expressive!

Top: Well, for a minute I thought you *did* mean it. I was almost ready to pack up. But I remembered that you've done this before, and I just waited. Those sobs *were* very convincing. Then you settled back to your "wishing" style and I knew I had better stick around. You'll *never* really get rid of me! Not fully!

Under: I WILL TOO! Or I hope I will. I want you out *so* badly. It felt good when I screamed at you. Even the sobbing relieved me. But I guess you're right. I'm not ready yet. It kind of scares me to think of being open and free. It's much safer with you around even though you do tie me up. Right now I feel a little less tense in my throat, but my shoulders still ache and my stomach has an even bigger knot which seems to be moving downward. I wish it would stop!

Leader: Have you ever resented anything? Have you ever felt like hitting something?

Under: Oh yes! I often have resentment of all kinds! But I never hit anything. I would be afraid to!

Leader: What would you fear?

Under: I might *hurt* somebody!

Leader: Would you be willing to hit that pillow—that large black leather one?

Under: I guess so. Yes!

Leader: Then put it out in front of you on the floor. Get down on your knees in front of it. Raise your arms high over your head, fists clenched, and hit the pillow as hard as you can. Like this. (Demonstrating.) Now you do it!

Under: (Takes position on knees in front of pillow. Hesitates. Finally hits it one rather gentle blow.) I guess I can't do it very well.

Leader: Would you be willing to say "won't" instead of "can't?" You haven't hit it very hard yet. It's my fantasy that you can and will when you want to!

Under: I guess you are right. I'll try again. (Hits pillow three or four half-hearted blows. Stops)

Leader: I noticed you stopped. Is that all you want to do?

Under: (Is silent on knees staring at pillow. Finally answers.) No, I don't believe so. But it feels so strange. I want to, but I can't—I mean it seems like I can't—like something is holding me back. And you I *do* want to continue!

Leader: Then continue!

(Under hits with renewed force, making a strong impact now. The blows make a resounding thud which seems to spur on Under to increase the force of her blows.)

Leader: Can you give your resentment a voice?

Under: (Stops hitting, a bit out of breath. Looks at leader.) What do you mean?

Leader: Your body is expressing your resentment silently, except for the thud of your blows. Can you let your voice out? Would you be willing to say "No!" or "I won't!" while you are hitting? If so, try again and let your voice out!

Under: (Resumes hitting much more violently now. Starts to speak. Softly, at first, then louder.) I won't! I won't! I won't! I WON'T! I WON'T! I WON'T! WON'T! WON'T! (Continues to hit for maybe five to ten minutes. During this time leader says "I WILL!" after each "I WON'T" of Under. The emotion rises to fever pitch. Finally Under collapses on the pillow breathing deeply, punctuated by sobs and tears. She lies there for a full ten to twelve minutes breathing deeply and sobbing occasionally. Then she gets up to her knees and looks at Leader.)

Leader: What are you experiencing now? What do you feel?

Under: I feel exhausted, out of breath, tired.

Leader: What's going on in your body?

Under: I'm tired, but I'm more relaxed. I feel better, I think. Right now I'm not sure. My arm muscles ache. I rubbed some skin off my hands.

Leader: What do you feel in your shoulders? Stomach?

Under: The ache in my shoulders is all gone. Less tension there. Stomach? I don't know. The knot is less knotty, less tense. Seems to want to go somewhere. Don't know where.

Leader: Are you all through? Do you want to do more?

Under: Yes I do! (Rearranges pillow so as to give it a more direct hit.)

Leader: This time continue as before—as loud and as long as you can. Also, open your eyes and focus on what you are hitting!

Under: (Kneeling with fists clenched, jaw set, on knees in front of pillow. Glares at pillow. Starts to hit.) I won't! I won't! I won't! I WON'T! I WON'T! (Continues much longer this time. Aggression increases to fever pitch. Voice much louder. Eyes glare at pillow, closing momentarily, and reopening with renewed fire. Voice finally develops a pleading quality. Pitch rises. Pleading increases, punctuated by sobs. Eyes close. Breathing gets deeper. Falls across pillow convulsed with sobs, murmuring softly "I won't. I won't." Finally is silent except for deep breathing. Lies silently for fifteen to seventeen minutes. Finally looks up. Hair is disheveled. Face is tear-stained. Face has lost its tense, fearful look, is much softer and relaxed now. Eyes are softer and more outward-looking. They make better contact with others. She returns to her seat slowly.)

Leader: And what are you experiencing *now*?

Under/Top: I no longer feel under. Somehow I seem to have gotten out. I feel much more relaxed. My arms and shoulders are very tingly, tired, and also relaxed, not tense. My throat is raw and hoarse, but I feel less neck tension in those muscles. My stomach? I still don't know. It's different, that's for sure. And the difference is an improvement. I feel sure it wants to tell me something, but I'm not sure what.

Leader: What were you hitting? A pillow—yes. But who or what was the pillow? What were you seeing as you hit the pillow?

Under/Top: This time I stared at the pillow. At first I only saw the black leather. Then a face appeared, a blank face. I didn't know whose it was. But it was leering at me, making fun of me and my efforts to hit. This infuriated me further and I glared at it even more. At times I seemed for a minute to know who it was, but not clearly. I only know it was taunting me, making fun of me. I hated it and wanted to destroy it! Maybe it was my topdog?

Leader: Maybe! At any rate if you continue this kind of activity, you may learn who it is, if this is important. What is important is your experiences, your feelings, and that you are on the way!

What you have just read is a rather typical example of an encounter—an encounter between the topdog and the underdog of one person. The leader facilitates the encounter at certain strategic points to help the subject keep the fire going. In doing this, he becomes a part of the encounter and must keep his part of it direct and clear so as to help the underdog to do her thing as fully as she actually wants to do it. At any point, should she want to withdraw or escape, she would be allowed to do so. However the leader would simply attempt to make her aware of what she is doing. He would also help her to realize that whatever she chooses to do is her own responsibility and therefore it can be whatever she wants it to be.

In this particular encounter, the beginning is pitched almost entirely at a verbal level. There is a minimum of overt signs of involvement except in the kinds of words spoken. Voices are calm if not swallowed in whispers. Facial expressions are blank. Body posture is stiff and withdrawn.

As the encounter proceeds, the topdog succeeds in needling the underdog into more forceful action, first in verbal resentment, then at a vocal level. Here the individual is doing the job of building her own involvement, using the format of the dialogue for this purpose.

After a certain point of emotional pitch and frustration, the dialogue leaves the purely verbal level. This is necessary, in this case, as the subject seems to be able to continually escape when the argument gets too heated. At these times, she escapes by playing the "Poor me!" game and *wishing* to be out rather than taking any steps to get out. The shouting makes it harder to escape involvement, but she still eventually does escape—in spite of sobs, tears, and screams. It is here that the encounter must become more physical if it is to produce any more resolution and insight.

With her own permission, the leader-facilitator moves the subject to the level of physical action. Here she increases her involvement as a result of direct physical action plus deep breathing and focused eye contact. She is able to encounter her "punisher" at a symbolic level, doing no physical damage to anyone or anything. At the same time, she frees her muscular blocks in throat, shoulders, and arms. This gets her more together than she was at the start. Underdog has come out from under quite a bit and is no longer pushed around. There is little, if any, pleading going on at the end.

"What has this to do with riding with feelings? How can an encounter be used to better 'control,' get on top of, and ride with feelings?"

Well, our subject in the encounter is full of feelings although many of them are repressed. Most of her conscious feelings are that she is trapped, compressed, squelched by some power or force beyond her

91

knowledge and beyond her control. As we have said repeatedly in other chapters, she is split and therefore does not know herself. She tends to look outside for her controller and to look outside for a way out. She may tend to blame other people or the world at large. "Why do *things* always go against me? Why do *they* make me so afraid?" With this approach, her feelings get even more intense and more unbearable. And her trap gets tighter and deeper. What is she to do?

We have said in chapter 6 that one must find a way to ride with feelings and, if possible, exaggerate them. The encounter is one way to do this. But unless one has had practice, it is necessary to have an experienced person to facilitate the process, to keep you constantly facing the issue at hand, taking responsibility for your actions and feelings, and not copping out. The method to be used is the one described at the beginning of the chapter, usually starting with a self-dialogue and ending with, or moving toward, overt physical action. In this way inner, somewhat hidden, feelings can come out and eventually be personified. The persons can each take their parts, and as this develops, feelings can be exaggerated to the heights of verbal and physical expression. In this way you become aware of what is going on inside of you and how the various persons of you are producing the feelings you are so troubled with. You ride the encounter to its fullest peaks until exhaustion calls a halt. You should be aware, however, that for most healthy persons, exhaustion is a cop-out. Most of us can stand more pain and go on much further than we say we can go. Our exhaustion and pain threshold are ways of avoiding deeper and more pervading levels of feelings and emotion. Notice that our subject in the sample encounter here continually increased her ability to go further by repeated trials—and without much rest in between. In repeating these attempts, she was gaining strength, putting herself together, and therefore *wanting* to go on and experience more. And the further she went, the more depth she experienced and the further she could go. Each attack caused her to ride further with her feelings. Each attack brought her closer to being in touch with her inner self.

"These examples and this discussion so far are all about encountering myself. I see that, and I see its usefulness. But what about encountering someone else? I encounter, or almost encounter, other people every day, and I seem to get nowhere. Largely this is because I am *afraid* of what would happen if we hit head on. So, I'm frank to say, I escape, I cop out, I dodge the issue. And we go along making out that it's all settled. Of course it isn't, and I end up all uptight. What can I do about this? Or do I just live with it?"

Again we must ask what do you *want* to do? Of course you can live with your escapes. But if they become objectionable and make you uptight, there are other approaches besides escape.

"Suppose my wife is a very sensitive person whom I understand very poorly, and I don't understand why. Suppose I feel her demands upon me are very great and unreasonable. Yet if I try to confront her with these 'facts,' she reacts as though she had been attacked or cruelly put down. I know that one approach is escape—just grit my teeth and *act* as though everything were all right, just to keep peace. But if I choose this route, I know I can expect chronic headaches, an early ulcer, or an acute heart ailment unless I have some outside way to release my tension in a physical way. But I can't just run over her sensitivities, can I?"

Yes, you can. But you needn't. You have described your wife quite well, but what are *you* like? What kind of repressed bulldozing mechanisms do you have? What are the needs you have which you aren't facing? One way to face her, is to face the *you in her*—the projections you are dumping on her. Could it be that her sensitivities are very necessary reactions on her part in order to survive with you?

You might confront her with your confrontation of yourself. If you have encountered yourself at all, as described above, you should gain some insights about yourself. You might present her with these—what you have learned about yourself, what kinds of changes you want to make in yourself, what you like about yourself. You might also tell her what situations cause you resentment—cause *you* to make *yourself* resentful. You might tell her ways you see yourself changing and see if she corroborates these. You can level with her *completely* about how *you* see *yourself* and how you feel about yourself. However when you approach her with the eye of a surgeon or as a diagnostician of *her* ailments, have caution! It is far better to escape *from* your analysis of her to your analysis of you. She may well help you with your self-analysis. Or she may just sit and listen and say, "Yes dear!" Later on, however she may encounter you with *her* self-analysis. She may tell you how she upsets herself, and what makes *her* resentful—how she makes *herself* resentful. In this encounter, you can help her, perhaps, and corroborate things she says, if she asks for this. It is wise to let her do her own self-analysis, however. Your analysis of her is too apt to be a projection to be valid, and your projection in *her* self-analysis is worse than sand in the vaseline! So you need not escape from encountering your wife. But don't confuse encountering her with dissecting her!

"What about encountering other people? My boss? My mother? My teacher? My friend? Can I level with them? Is it always a matter of dealing with *me*? Can I ever tell them how I feel toward *them*—what irks or irritates me about *them*?"

Of course you can with profit encounter anyone. But ask yourself what is really going on. Is it just a release of pent up emotion? Do you just want a target for your aggressions? If so, perhaps a pillow is a better means to this end. If you have a friend who can (and will) take your shit, perhaps this is acceptable. But in most cases dumping one load of shit just leads to another load back. This has questionable value and usually leads to more pent-upness than you started with. This is particularly true if there is no "umpire" for the encounter. For this reason reciprocal exchanges of hostility are usually best done in a group where feed-back is available to help the two parties to the encounter to see themselves more realistically. In a group situation, someone must be on hand to prevent a mass scapegoating of one or the other of the parties to the exchange, and often this is a most delicate situation to handle. Usually the solution is for someone with experience to call to each person's attention what he is observed as doing, give him feedback on his behavior, and see how he reacts to this. This may quiet or dilute his violent accusations of his opponent and give him insights with a broader perspective. The feedback may also help to turn aside any mass attacks on any one individual. The simple question, "How do you now feel about what you just said?" can have a very salutory effect. It turns the focus from other to self. The fire is in your house now! For these reasons group encounters are to be highly recommended when conducted by a skillfully trained person. In the group context, violence of a direct personal nature can be directed constructively and seen in a broader perspective. Violence can also be dramatized, and role-played, and released as was shown at the beginning of this chapter.

"Suppose I do not want a target for my aggressions? Suppose I just want to exchange ideas, share feelings, or get a broader understanding? What then?"

Of course these are worthy and necessary desires. But, again, are you using your partner as a means to your ends? Or do you enjoy your partner and his reactions, just as they are? Do you covertly hope to change him in some way through the encounter? Are you aware which of these possibilities is true of you?

Here again, it would profit you to encounter your self in these regards, and *then* to engage in your encounter with the other person. The encounter may then be more profitable to you both.

What has been said so far is true regardless of who the other person to the encounter is. It is wise to consider your own purposes before going into any encounter, if possible. It is even wise to dialogue on this subject with the two or more sides of yourself before going into the encounter. This will sensitize you to the other. It will boil off any high pressure steam as well.

It is wise to consider that your "opponent" has human sensitivities (such as the wife in the example above). If you do, you are more likely to make your approach with due regard for these. Here it must be clear that you are not just subjugating yourself to someone else's tenderness. You are not letting this request for tenderness dominate you. However if you feel the desire to press, you must avoid the bulldozer approach. You must avoid acting as though it were your *right* to be as rough to this "natural terrain" as you care to be. You must clarify what you want to get from this encounter and attempt to act in terms of these desires.

"But how can I remember all this crap? When I get into an encounter, it comes on the spur of the moment. I don't have *time* for all this!"

Yes, I know. You will make mistakes. You will trample, you will scapegoat, you will use others for your own purposes. But you do not have to repeat these mistakes. If you encounter yourself after one of these "mistakes," you may get a little insight. With this insight you can practice your encounter alone, talking as though your opponent were present, in the same style described in the beginning of the chapter. If you do this, you will gain more skill. And when you are again in an encounter—even on the spur of the moment—you will be more spontaneous and do much better.

We see, then, that encounters are affairs of the feelings. They take place now, in the present, never then. In an encounter I can touch. I touch me—the two sides of myself—and with this touch I become whole. I get in touch with my inner self. I can touch others, and by this means I come together with them and see myself even more clearly. We are often told to escape disagreeable encounters. They are often painful, hard to take. But unless I choose to be split, sick or apart, I will not knowingly escape an encounter. I will, however, approach it lovingly with the same kind of respect as I would a person. For in an encounter new persons may be born and old persons may be reborn. The furnace of the encounter softens the human metal and allows it to reform itself. In an encounter I can make me or remake me. You can make you or remake you. But you and I cannot ever make or remake each other.

11

The Encounter
As a Way
of
Wrestling with God

And Jacob was left alone;
and there wrestled a man with him
until the breaking of the day

"When I am alone, I sometimes feel very small. I am by myself, apart, with no one else, with nothing else. My world, my surroundings, seem very frightening and vast. I am tiny by comparison. And I feel afraid.

"At such times I am not split. My tiny self is all one. But it is an unknown one, a strange one. I am afraid of what is in it, in *me*, and I sit in my aloneness and shiver in the cold of the dark night.

"My possessions are apart from me, 'across the river.' As I sit there in the night alone, I have a powerful urge to find someone else to break my aloneness. And I also have the driving passion to know this person who sits there in the dark, to go inside of me and see the light.

"And so I wrestle in my wilderness with the God which is within me. We struggle through the night, He and I. At length He touches me, 'touches my thigh,' and it is most painful. However I do not give up. I will not let Him go until the day dawns and I can see His face—until I can see the unity, the holiness, the godliness, which is me.

"After this struggle, I limp a bit all the next day. But the pain is very satisfying. For I am now a new person. I no longer need to

97

hide and shrink as I did before. I am touched by God and I can feel His touch as I limp. He touches me *now*. And I know that should my tininess return, I can always return to my wilderness and fast, and wrestle, and see His face—my own inner face—and in this way be strengthened and made holy. This I will need to do whenever God's touch becomes a memory and not a *now*!"

The speaker above is speaking of an encounter, but a far different one from the one discussed in the last chapter. In the last chapter there were two forces, Top and Under, each trying to be successful in winning out against the other. Top is the controller, the punisher, the squelcher. Under is the pleader, the escaper. Under wants to get out and run away (he says). Top wants to dominate and call Under's bluff. The resolution of this encounter is the coming together of Top and Under in a head-on confrontation, with Under finally getting out and being self-sufficient and responsible for his actions. In the confrontation, feelings are expressed to the fullest and healing and understanding come about, in part, through the intense expression of these feelings.

In the encounter above, there is no real split into two persons or two selves. There is one person who does not know himself and is afraid to know himself. He does not have two persons to *get together*. He has one self to *get into*, to get in touch with. To go *in* and get in touch is a real struggle, however. It is far easier to go *out* and seek someone else to be concerned with. But in the process of wrestling and going *in*, I get in touch with my deeper experiences. I get to know my inner self. I get to know the God which is within me. I feel renewed and touched by these deeper experiences in a very strengthening way.

This is the kind of encounter that must eventually take place alone. Someone else may start me on the road and give me a helping hand along the way. But no one else can direct it. No one else can tell me how. I must go off by myself in my own wilderness. I must leave my material possessions behind, in the sense that they are not in my mind. I must leave "food" behind and fast, in the sense that I am not concerned with my appetite—gastronomic or psychological. I must leave my superficial behavior behind—my habits, my passing fancies, my ideas. I must leave my sensory impressions behind. I must even leave my goals and my desires. I, only, am with me. I can, then, face, go into, and get in touch with that core which is the center of what I really am.

"But I have never done this kind of thing at all! It all sounds so mysterious, so religious. I usually try to be with people—at least one good friend or member of my family—whenever I want to experience things deeply. Their company, their confirmation is most calming and gives me a feeling of great warmth and security. Why should I give up this companionship? Are you saying that the best things in life are those you experience alone?"

Of course, your pattern of experiencing has to be your own. You choose it. You make it what you want it to be. But you need not be stuck with this pattern. You can extend it and vary it in ways which may be most rewarding. To wrestle alone may sound mysterious but perhaps only because it is different from your usual pattern of experience. It is religious in the sense that religious things are those associated with higher and deeper experiences. It is *not* religious in that you must be bound to it in an institutionalized sense—you must hold strictly to certain values and ideas and no others. Your God, your conception of God, is your belief in your deeper and more involving experiences—those experiences that are most truly you and that you value above all else. These are the roots of your being. These are where you really live. To get to these experiences, to come to grips with yourself—your God—is a matter of aloneness. But when you have returned from your wilderness, you will want to share your experiences—your holiness—with others. Hopefully you will not want to do this kind of sharing to *convert* anyone else to your way of life, but simply to form a bond with them. More often your sharing will be implicit in your whole attitude toward others. You will not—you can not—tell about your encounter with God. But the results will show in the way you relate to others. You will be more secure, more authentic. And the aspect of deep security is undeniable. "My how you have changed!" they will say. "You seem so much more at ease and at peace with things! How did you do it?" In part you did it alone. But you need not, and should not, give up experiences with others. These can be very nourishing and rewarding. And after being alone, you will profit from your associations even more than before. You will know better how to avoid, or quickly terminate, toxic relationships and how to cherish and cultivate nourishing ones. In this way you will also be more rewarding to your companions. They will see you and know you more clearly and you can nourish them more fully. These associations and contacts with others are very important kinds of touches in your life. But they must not be all. They need to be punctuated by the trips of fasting in the wilderness. The art of life is how to balance these two types of experiences so as to have them be of greatest mutual benefit.

"But how can *I* achieve your type of security? How can I also become authentic? I feel so empty at times. I need to have a more centered life. But I do not know how to do it. I need to know who I am, not just who I want people to *think* I am!"

Of course I cannot prescribe in detail exactly what you should do. It is your life, and you must be the prescriber. You could not follow my style even if you wanted to. But I can suggest some ways, situations, and techniques that might help you to prescribe for yourself.

Let us assume you are relatively whole, healthy, and together as a result of following what was described in chapter 10. If this is so, you have no internal war going on. You are willing to be responsible for your actions, and you know what that means. You might start then by keeping a journal of your reactions, feelings, thoughts, and wishes about yourself. Write in it at least once every day or whenever you have a chance to do so. Be as free and full in writing your entries as you can and do not cross out or erase any part of any entry. If a sentence or word does not please you, simply write "I don't like what I just wrote." In this way you will begin a running account of what you are and how you grow and develop.

With this procedure well underway, schedule yourself for at least one hour of "alone time" *each day*. This you may want to increase, but it should never be less than one hour. Of course, if you are like Mr. or Mrs. John Q. American, you probably have zero hours of alone time per week and maybe not more than one or two such hours a month.

In your alone time, there should be *absolutely nothing* which you have to accomplish or produce. You are, first and foremost, alone. You are not traveling anywhere. You are not eating. You are not about to sleep. You are not bathing. You are not planning something. You are simply alone with yourself, and you have ruled out all productive activity. There is nothing for you to accomplish here. You are in the wilderness alone! One of the great problems will be *where*, in what physical space, will you have your alone time? This you must solve, and I am sure if you want it badly enough, you can find such a place.

Let us assume you have such a place, and you are beginning your alotted hour. What to do? Immediately turn *in* on yourself. A fantasy might help. "I am on a high mountain road. It leads in a circular fashion around the side of a huge mountain. To my left is a deep precipice. It extends hundreds of feet down into a valley full of grass, farm houses, and livestock. To my right is the rocky face of the mountain. It is sheer and solid and greyish-black in color. Ahead of me is the road, rutted and rough with occasional boulders blocking the path so that I have to climb over them to go ahead.

"What feelings do I have? I feel a deep foreboding. I am fearful as I look down, although the cool green of the valley is inviting. The rock wall to my right repulses me, yet it is less scary than the precipitous drop to my left. The road ahead is singularly uninviting. Where does it go? Why am I on it? Why did I leave that valley? I am a mass of regrets and premonitions. I do not like where I am at all!"

Or the fantasy might be of another type. "I am riding along the coast highway. It is a beautiful day and I am alone. The sky is blue, clear, and flecked with a few fluffy white clouds. I can see the blue expanse of the ocean to my right. I park my car as near as I can get to the ocean and hurry down a path to the beach. I take off my shoes and socks and stand in the warm, dry sand. Before me is the ocean, waves rushing in and breaking over the rocks just off shore. I see a few sea gulls above the rocks. They occasionally swoop down to the water for a fish and give out their raucous cry. The sand is almost white and very fine. I wiggle my toes as I walk along and finally decide to sit down against a large rock and take in the scene.

"What do I feel? I feel excited by the scene but secure and at ease. I love the rise and fall of the ocean and the anomalous pattern of the waves as they come in and recede again. The sea gulls interest me, but I am glad they keep their distance. The sand is warm and smooth. I feel very much at home and wonder why I have stayed away so long!"

These are only two examples. They are not models, so do not copy them. They are ways of starting on alone time just to see what happens. The result is unimportant at first, so long as there is no product. The time is spent purely on self-experience. Before the alone time is over, take time to be attentive to your feelings and at the very end ask yourself, "I have many feelings and sensations. But these are not all of me. What else am I?"

Of course alone time may be started *any* way which is non-productive—nonproduct oriented. It can simply start with a feeling survey as was described in chapter 9. This could easily continue for 45 minutes and leave enough time to pull it all together and come up with an approach to the question above, "What else am I?"

Alone time might be started with a belief survey. "What do I believe about life? What do I believe about other people? What do I believe about money? About sex? About war? About education? What do I believe about myself?" And finally, "These are my beliefs. But they are not all of me. What else am I?"

On another occasion I might simply do a thought survey. Let a thought come dancing in across my mind. Let it move and grow and accumulate feelings with it as it goes. Let it be displaced by, or lead to, other thoughts. Let these thoughts flow naturally, freely, without control. Again ask the question, "These are some of my thoughts, and I have many more. But they are not all of me. What else am I?"

These kinds of surveys can be conducted in other areas of experience. Visual awareness can be used in this way. "I am aware of the yellow color on the wall. I am aware of the glint on the window pane. I am aware of the gold color of the carpet. I am aware of the red color of the tile." Or, "I hear a motor sound. I hear a humming sound. I hear vocal music. I hear coughing." Either of these can be continued almost without end and will also generate their own feelings. The final question is again, "But these are not all of me. What else am I?"

As you spend more and more hours in alone time, you will want to let the flow of your experiences go further and deeper into each one. Eventually you will want to go through all the dimensions of your experience, peeling off one layer at a time to see what is underneath. You may start with the visual, move to the auditory, then to the feeling level, starting with what seems most external and going to what seems to be at a deeper level. Of course you will report all your feelings and reactions to these alone time sessions in your journal. And at least once a week you will read over your entries and attempt to sum up what you are *now*!

All of these alone time activities are designed to put you in closer touch with what is going on within you. As you do this, you will see more clearly the various subpersonalities within you. And you will also come into closer touch with that inner self, to which we have referred so often, and which is the potential organizer of all your experiences and of all your various subordinate selves. This is the God within you who can be your creative organizer. This is the God whom you touch and wrestle with. This is also the self that can unite you with other persons outside yourself.

In presenting the material above, I am drawing heavily from the work of Roberto Assagioli and Robert Gerard. The book, *Psychosynthesis,* by Dr. Assagioli (on which Dr. Gerard collaborated) is a rich source of inspiration and contains a great wealth of other activities that may be carried out if you wish to get in closer touch with your inner self.

But all this is preliminary to your real trip to the wilderness. For you will eventually come to areas of your experience—of your self—which are most painful to contemplate. Or you will come to other areas where you are filled with great doubt about what you are. "Can I really be a person who controls and dominates so joyfully? I always felt I was tender, gentle, and kind. What *am* I!?" Or "Am I really so tight-fisted and grasping? Do material things mean that much to me? I always felt I was generous and most willing to give. I always felt I could do without material advantages. What kind of a person *am* I!?"

When this occurs, when the pain is great enough, you will need to put aside all of your possessions, feelings, ideas, etc. You will need to put them "across the river" from yourself. You will need to cancel all of your agenda and prepare to wrestle with your God for however long it takes. It will be painful. It will be difficult. And you may not get full resolution in your first real encounter with God. But once you have opened up this avenue, you can go back to it again and again.

Once you have arrived at the core of your being, once you have touched and been touched by God, you can prepare to rebuild your self. You can sit on the rock where you wrestled and put together, around your core, the kind of person you want to be. You know you are responsible for your feelings, your perceptions, your ideas, your beliefs, your desires. You know you have various subpersonalities within you. And you can put all these together around your core in the fashion and style you desire to have. You can make of yourself and your life what you will! You *can* design your experiences. You also know that you will need to touch God again and again. You will not forget that you have wrestled with God. For as you walk, you will feel God's touch on your thigh and you will know you can see His face again when the confusion of your life makes it necessary.

12

The Encounter
As a Way
of
Teaching

Men must be taught as if you taught them not,
And things unknown proposed as things forgot.

We are all teachers. We love to show and tell. We love to guide and instruct. We love to furnish others with knowledge. We love to build a structure into their lives.

We do not need to be in a school to do this. We do not need a room, a building, a book, a blackboard, or even a schedule or lesson-plan to do it. All we need is one other person who will listen, ask, let us guide. All we need is someone who will follow.

There are many of us who are obvious in our teaching. There are parents who would like to guide their children. There are the teachers in schools. There are clergymen who would lead their congregations. There are doctors who would prescribe for their patients. There are statesmen who would influence citizens. There are salesmen who would sell to their customers—and many others.

But there are others of us who teach in less obvious ways. We tell of our travels and recommend where to go and not to go. We describe our good and bad fortune at stores, restaurants, theaters, and service agencies. We advocate books and literature of all kinds. And we pan those we don't like. We discuss our social contacts, the "dates" we have had, and the parties we have attended. We describe, fully, the personalities of individuals we have met and freely give of our opinions and recommendations about them. We discuss and display our style of dress and mode of living and, although we do not want to be copied, we would be glad to be followed in these regards. In all these ways, and many others, we seek to guide and instruct others throughout our daily lives. In this respect we are teachers of those who come within our orbit.

Let us notice that in all these examples, there is some kind of encounter taking place. Persons are meeting face-to-face, and there must also be an exchange of words, feelings, ideas—although the flow is usually greater away from than toward the "teacher." Let us notice that there must also be some kind of touching going on. There is touch in the sense that the "teacher" is (it seems) bringing about changes in the bodies of the "students." They become excited, bored, angered, interested, or calmed. We saw in chapters 2 and 3 that it is a moot question as to who is responsible for these touches, these bodily feelings. But regardless of this debatable point, there is an encounter in teaching, and like all encounters, it involves touch. We will see later on that the kind of touch is very important in determining the kind of teaching going on.

Now, while we are all teachers, we are only slightly aware of *what* we teach. As in school, one must ask the students to find out what a teacher is really teaching. Miss Chalkdust, who supposedly teaches English, may in fact be teaching how unsure she is of her sexual identification. Mr. Straightjacket, a geometry teacher according to the schedule, may be teaching how necessary it is for him to be in control. And so it goes. As a rule, the teacher himself is almost totally unaware of what he is teaching; but the students would agree, with almost one voice, what the teacher's lesson really is. Let us look at a few of the teachers we meet in everyday life, and see what they are really "putting down."

"I hear you're going to Mexico, Marilyn. Well just let me tell you where to go. I know you haven't been there, and you know George and I just got back. We know all the interesting places to go to—where to eat, where to stay, what to see. You will love it! Don't worry about any of the details. I have it all worked out for you.

"You say Bob doesn't want to go? Well you better let him know which side his bread is buttered on. You have to be firm with men and make then live up to their commitments. He told you you were going this summer, didn't he? Well don't let him back down now! I know you have been planning for it a long time. He owes it to you! It's the least he can do after all you have done for him all these years.

"By the way, if you are going to buy any clothes for your trip, don't go to Fancy Threads—you know, that store on Main Street. I bought a dress there for our trip, and the seam came out after I had worn it just once! I was really burned up! There is a much better shop in Bay City. I buy all my clothes there now. I'll take you up there tomorrow and show you around. I know you will simply *love* their selection of clothes! They have just the things that would look good on you. I'll call you about ten and we can have lunch at that cute little Japanese restaurant before we shop! You'll love the food and it's very reasonable too. Goodbye, dear, and don't forget what I said about Bob!"

This is the pontiff speaking! She is the authority on all things personal, material, or gastronomic. She loves to be the authority on all subjects and as such is also the corrector of all errors—other people's, that is. She never makes any of her own. She sees herself as the source of knowlege for all her friends and tells them how she loves to help. However she has an insatiable desire to control. By being an authority, she can satisfy this desire very easily. Undoubtedly her husband is already fully subjugated. And her children, if she has any, have all passed the age where her influence can have any more effect. Hence her need to control must be exercised outside of her family.

She sees herself as counselor and advisor to her friends and acquaintances. A few of these "students" will agree with her and claim she is very helpful to them. Others will see her as a parent whom they cannot do without but who, incidentally, keeps them immature. Most of her "students" will hate her guts and reject or ridicule her efforts, calling her a controlling, know-it-all bitch! Her touch is always velvety on the outside but in the velvet glove is a hand of iron. It is gentle only on the surface, for, above all; it is the touch of control. When her touch (her control) is rejected she usually leaves the scene and tries to "excommunicate" the recalcitrant one at the same time. She essentially teaches others her great need to control, and she will continue an encounter only as long as she is in control.

"Well, thank God the remodeling of our house is finally completed! That makes it three thousand square feet—almost half again larger than it was before! This will be much more comfortable for us. The living room will be almost twice as large and the new master bedroom and bath are each fifty percent larger. Our entire house now is a third larger than our old one was. I don't know how we ever lived under those conditions!

"Oh, yes, it was quite expensive. The builder told me we would have to pay between five and ten thousand to do the job right, and what do you think? It cost *over* ten thousand! Why that's more than I used to make in a year! But I guess that shows how things are increasing.

"The houses around ours are nice too. But most of them are smaller—two thousand to twenty-five hundred square feet, I guess. The only other large house is the big white one with pink trim. It sits off by itself. Must be over four thousand feet! I bet it cost much more than ours, though. Looks to be a very expensively built house—all wood and glass. Ours will be much more economical to heat. I wonder why they picked that pink! Only flagrantly ostentatious people would do that. You know the kind I mean. You can always tell them by their houses, their cars, and the clothes they wear!"

Listen to El Comparator Supremo! He compares everything to see how well he can play the "bigger than" game or the "fits better than" game. He can only be secure if he and his are bigger and more fitting than all others around. He is very vocal, since he must continually broadcast his status. His "lesson" (he thinks) is to show his superiority as well as the superiority of his family and possessions. He spends a lot of time "teaching" this—and a lot of words too!

This speaker sees everything in comparisons. Cars are compared by cost, horse power, and size; clothes and houses by cost; education by cost and number of years spent; paintings by cost and size. And so it goes. One wonders if his honeymoon was measured by cost, length, or number of orgasms—or was it how well it fit with the existing style in such things?

He is obviously insecure about himself. His comparisons are his framework for trying to achieve security. But it doesn't work. Something else is always bigger and better. Almost all of his "students" know of his insecurity—and also how deadly boring he is to be with for any length of time. He has a suspicion of his lack of rapport with others, but he puts it down as jealousy on their part. What else can he do? He must teach, even though his lesson is self-defeating. He convinces few, if any, of his high status, and he must continually give much of his energy to broadcasting and to increasing and "improving" whatever he owns. His encounters are always on an unequal basis—to see who is bigger and better. His touch is a comparator's touch—to feel the other's roughness and lack of quality. Hence it is always judgmental. He never touches just for enjoyment. Enjoyment would be too deeply involving and too personal. It would focus on the self that he wants to escape so badly in his comparisons.

"But what has all this to do with teaching? Are you really serious that these people are teaching anything to anybody? You have simply described two obviously objectionable personality types (which I have known all too frequently) and shown how they operate. They spout a lot. But I don't call this teaching. And I am not sure they really encounter or touch anybody either."

Well you have a point there. But would you not say these people were trying to influence and guide the behavior of others? The pontiff wants to control. The comparator wants to show his personal superiority. In this sense they are trying to "teach" others. Do they encounter others? Yes, in a way, although their encounters are often oblique. They are rarely face-to-face because these individuals are not willing to let the other one see or have access to them fully. Do they touch? I believe so—even a repulsive touch is still a touch. It produces a reaction in the body. But let's listen to another type of teaching situation.

"Hi Bill, am I glad I saw you! I called you three times today. Couldn't get you at all. Do you have a minute?"

"Sure, Dick, sit down. I was just going to leave, but I could use another cup of coffee. Glad to have somebody to talk to. What's on your mind?"

"Well, do you remember my daughter, Sally? She's in a terrible mess, and I don't know what to do about it. I thought maybe you could help. You have a daughter too. I believe she's married now, isn't she?"

"Yes, Linda has been married for almost a year now. But what's the problem?"

"Well, Sally has been going with this guy for almost two years, ever since high school, and it's really getting serious. But the problem is that he doesn't want to work or go to school. He is very gentle and considerate of Sally—very loving too, I guess. But he just seems to sponge off her and the money she gets from us. He doesn't have a car—at least not one that runs very well. So they always use ours. If they go out, she usually pays the bill. And now they are *really* getting emotionally involved. They are together almost every weekend—at the beach or the mountains and often by themselves. Of course Sally knows all about birth control, but we were afraid for her to take the pill, and what if that "device" doesn't work? We'd be stuck with an indigent son-in-law to support. I swear Mary and I lie awake for hours some nights worrying about it!"

"What is the worst that could happen, Bill? What's the worst catastrophe you could imagine, as far as Sally is concerned?"

"Well I guess it would be Sally getting pregnant and having to marry that guy."

"And how would you feel about that? Would you want her to marry him under those conditions?"

"Yes, I guess I would. But we could always have her get an abortion, or even put the kid up for adoption."

"Have you talked this over with Sally? How does she feel about such a prospect?"

"Sally feels there's no chance of her getting pregnant unless she wants to. She doesn't know what we are worrying about. And she says what George (that's his name) does is his own business and hers—and *not ours!* She doesn't realize that at present it's we who are just about supporting them both!"

"What would you like to happen as far as Sally is concerned?"

"Well, I don't really know. I want her to be happy and have a good family and a secure homelife. I want her to have love. And I want her to have children—if and when she wants them. And I want her to have a husband who can take care of her and the children too!"

"And how do you feel about George in this regard?"

"Like I said, he doesn't want to work or go to school. He does love Sally and he's good to her. But my God, Bill, a guy just has to earn money, doesn't he?"

"Have you ever talked to George about this, Dick?"

"Not really. Sally gets embarrassed whenever we try to talk to the kid (he's only twenty); and when we do, she always defends him. Says he's making up his mind how to live life, and that's what more of *us* ought to do. She says it is adults who have screwed up the world so kids like them can't live a decent, honest life. She says it's the adult world which continually fucks up kids minds and lives!"

"And how do you answer that?"

"I don't! I just *burn* and usually leave the room. Why when I was twenty I was working hard at a job and going to school too! Of course, I missed out on a lot of the fun and good times some of my buddies had. But I saved money, and when Mary and I wanted to get married, we were all set! Imagine! Telling us *we* screwed *them* up! Why we laid a foundation for them! We gave them everything! And even now we are just about supporting them both. What, in God's name, do they want?"

"Did you ever ask them?"

"Well, now that you mention it, I guess not. Do you think I should? I wonder what they would say?"

"Well that just sounds like a couple of guys shooting the breeze with each other. One asks the questions. The other runs off at the mouth about his daughter. I don't call that teaching at all!"

But you would have to admit there is an encounter going on. Every time Dick starts to get off on a tirade, Bill throws him back to facing the question at hand. I would agree this is not teaching of the kind which goes on in most classrooms. It is certainly not like the teaching of the pontiff or comparer. But is there any guiding or instructing going on?

"Certainly not! Bill doesn't really guide Dick at all! He never tells him what to do. He doesn't even point out how wrong he is to push his daughter around like that. That Dick makes me so impatient! I just wanted to shake him to open his eyes. *I* could give him a few answers. Why I'd..."

Wait a minute! We're not here to set Dick straight. We're here to talk about teaching and encountering, remember? You sound like you would like to control Dick—just like the pontiff. Is there no other way?

"Well, I don't know of any. Guiding seems to me to mean giving answers, or at least suggestions. Instructing seems to me to mean indicating methods of doing things. If you can't give Dick any answers, at least you can show him *how* to deal with his daughter!"

But do you suppose Dick would accept these answers? Would he follow new methods of dealing with Sally?

"Probably not. He's too hardheaded and stiff-necked. But what else could be done?"

Well, if Dick won't take answers or follow new methods we, at least, know what *not* to do. We don't give him any. And I suspect many of us are more like Dick than we care to admit. We want to do it *our* way, find our *own* answers, use our *own* methods which *we* have devised. If this is true, to teach *answers* and *methods* which the "student" has had *no part* in getting is to have the lesson backfire. Nothing is learned. There must, then, be another method—a method where the student can *find his own* answers and *devise his own* methods of operation. He can hardly do this alone, or he would have solved his problem long ago. *The fact that someone has had a problem for some time indicates the need for help.* So to teach in this other way would mean, at least, not to give answers or prescribe any methods. It would also mean to call the attention of the student to what is going on in him and in the situation, and to gently help him to face the problem at hand whenever his attention slips away in an emotional digression. It would also mean to temporarily suppress the personal needs of the teacher to express *his* feelings about whatever the student was concerned with unless his feelings were explicitly called for. This can all be done in an encounter where the parties at hand face each other and the situation squarely. Can you see this going on at all with Bill and Dick?

"Yes, I guess so. Bill does call him back to the problem many times. But will Dick ever get any answers?"

I don't know. But at least this way, if he does, he is much more likely to believe them and use them. He is much more likely to use methods

111

he has devised too. And if he doesn't get any answers or methods right away, is he any worse off than rejecting someone else's?

"I guess not. But it all sounds like you are suggesting that we must teach by not teaching. That may be right, but it's certainly confusing."

Well let's go back again to some other examples of teaching. And let's keep Bill and Dick in mind as we do this and see if we come up with any ways to approach their problem.

"I never had much success in school. It was because my parents didn't care about school and because we never had any books at home for me to read. Then, too, I was always sickly as a child. This was because we all ate the wrong food and had very little access to modern preventative medical methods.

"When I got older and went to high school, I was still somewhat sickly. I tried to build myself up, but I just couldn't do it. My mother had babied me so long I couldn't stand on my own two feet. Of course it is easy to see why she did this. She had lost a child in a horrible accident before I was born and the memory of this never left her. She cried and cried at that time, but the shock was too great. It was the intensity of the shock and the fact that this child was her first son which made it so hard for her to deal with.

"In college I was healthier. I tried out for football then, but the coaches all wanted people with high school experience, so I never had a real chance—even though by then I was big and strong and quite well coordinated.

"Now I am an adult and I have recurrent headaches which I doctor with aspirin. They come at odd times, usually when I have to pay all my bills or am worried about other problems. I am sure I shall have them as long as I worry! But I wonder why I worry so much?"

We have just listened to the "explainer." His two favorite words are "why" and "because." He seems to know the reasons for almost everything and loves to give them. His lesson is, "I know everything. If I don't, I will find out." When he doesn't know why, he is sure to ask, as he does at the end of his statement. What his students learn is his lack of involvement and his distance from them. He rarely seems to be concerned with "how." One gets the idea that he may think that when he has found out why, he can control the situation. This is, of course, questionable. Suppose it is true that my mother overprotected me because of an accident to my older brother. How does this help me to change the situation now?

His neglect of "how" is just as serious as his overemphasis on "why." If he were concerned enough to describe in detail the situations and events he talks about, he might be able to get some new insights about them. He might start to understand the feelings which were generated in him by these events. For instance if I describe my mother's overprotection in all of its details, it is likely to conjure up feelings in me *now*. These feelings can make the overprotection real to me so that I can get in touch with it. I can see just how I resent it even now; and as I get in touch with these feelings, I can develop ways of dealing with them.

"But isn't it a good idea to seek for causes? I thought this is the way scientists work.They look for causes. Then they can make a plan, based on this understanding, to modify the situation in a desirable way."

Of course causes are interesting and sometimes helpful to know. However it is often impossible to objectively determine what is *the* cause in any particular human situation. In coming up with the cause, the investigator may fall into the trap of rationalizing his own values. On the other hand, the emphasis on "how," described in detail, often results in insights which lead implicitly to desirable, nearly automatic changes. When I "see" how things operate in me, I automatically change. I do not need to take time to "plan" to institute changes in my behavior.

Another important point is the fact that the objective determination of causes decidedly cools off the degree of involvement in the encounter between "teacher" and "student." To be objective we must talk about things in general—and no *real* person is a person in general. I can identify only with great difficulty with a person in general. I can truly identify only with a particular person. And this particular person must be as subjectively described as possible. Such subjectivity heightens the involvement of the encounter. Hence the focus on "how" increases involvement. The focus on "why" reduces it. For these reaons the explainer often loses the prize of closeness with his students. His touch is very cold. His encounter with his students is distant and minimal.

113

"I am glad you are getting along better with Phil now, Dolly. I was glad to talk with you both last Sunday morning. I wish you would feel free to call on me at any time. I consider you both my good friends, and any time I can help I am more than willing to do so.

"Would you like to have lunch with me tomorrow? I have a little shopping to do, but I can always do it another day. I am sure there are other things you might like to talk over face to face.

"What's that? Your car is broken down? Well don't let that bother you a minute. I can pick you up for lunch, and I can leave my car with you. I really don't need to use it. I can get a lift from my neighbor the few days I need to get to town. I know you just *have* to have a car to get to work, and I know you wouldn't want to burden Phil with the extra miles to get you there. I'll call you back to see exactly when you want me to pick you up. And don't forget, call me at any hour if you need me!"

This, of course, is the "helper" who considers all others before herself and ministers to their needs. Yes, she enjoys it. This is the way she keeps her friends, she thinks. And this is the way she keeps from attending to herself. If she is busy helping and considering others, she need not look at or listen to herself. This is painful to do, probably because she does not like herself very well.

Her lesson is, "I am always ready to help you, all of you, and I never run out of sympathy." Some of her students may learn just this. They may turn to her regularly and be thankful for her. Others, however, may exploit her and almost milk her dry in the process. Still others are repulsed by her interfering hovering—her super-overconcern.

"Isn't it good to help? Do unto others as you would have them do unto you. This seems pretty true to me."

You are right. Helping is almost like love. It makes the world go around. But perhaps the best way to help another person is to be sure your own house is in order, and if not, to put it in order. Then too, the best help is always given on request, in response to an expressed need by someone, and when the helper genuinely wants to give it. To force help on anyone is rarely appreciated. It leads to exploitation of the helper. To give help begrudgingly is also bad. It always can be sensed. Either of these can cause unexpressed hostility and resentment on the part of both helper and helped. I don't want your car. I blame you for pushing it on me. I sense you really don't want to lend it. And you resent my lack of gratitude. The worst part is that rarely can these feelings be expressed by either party. So they fester and cause little pools of toxicity. They are probably also displaced on other innocent persons in irrational ways. The helper ends up not being helpful or considerate. His touch is cloying and oppressive. His encounters with his students are slippery and without any real teeth. After a time one even gets the idea that the helper may not be altruistic at all!

We have seen, then, four kinds of teaching—the pontiff (or controller), the comparer, the explainer, and the helper. These are but four of the many which could be mentioned. They all teach something, even if their lesson is often not what they *really* teach. They all touch after a fashion, and their touch is a clue to what their lesson really is—the touch of camouflaged hardness, the touch of judging, the touch of coldness, the touch of cloying oppression.

None of these four really encounters his students or himself in a head-on fashion. There is always a lack of equality, a lack of closeness, or a lack of real engagement.

"But you have forgotten the fifth example of teaching—the example of Bill and Dick. You said you were coming back to them!"

So we did, and here we are. Let's reread their encounter and let's ask some questions about them. How would you compare Bill and Dick's experience with the four other examples of teaching? Was their encounter generally sharp and was it turned in a head-on direction whenever it tended to be oblique? Is it Bill who does this? Or does Dick help too? How would you describe Bill's touch? Gentle, controlling, punishing, placating, or explaining? Is Bill really teaching anything? If so, what is his lesson? What would Dick say about this? What would you say if you were Dick?

Whatever your opinion about these matters, it is our contention that a full head-on encounter is the ground from which the best teaching can grow. It is where teacher and student can grow as individuals, growing at different rates according to no one else's expectations. More diluted and oblique encounters also produce teaching. But here growth is hampered by built-in inequalities or lack of involvement. Touching in a true head-on encounter is never in doubt. It is felt by all concerned. It is due to this very evident touching that the teaching develops. It is here that teacher and student touch each other reciprocally. Each leaves his mark on the other and, as with Jacob, each knows that he can renew the encounter whenever it is needed—at his own demand and not at the demand of another.

13

What Did You Learn
in
School Today?

"Who do you have for English this semester, Holly?"

"I have Mr. Wordsworthless. I really hate that class. He is so proper. I bet he couldn't say 'shit' if he had a mouth full of it. He goes on and on and on about literature and grammar and his kind of poetry. He doesn't seem to know about Bob Dylan or John Lennon. They are poets too! I wonder what he really expects us to do in that class, just *listen* to him? The only time we really get to talk is when he calls on us. Then he ridicules us if we mispronounce a word or say something wrong. *His* answers are the only right ones!

"Do we have written assignments? Do we ever? At least one a week—story, essay, or something else. I just hate to do them. It's not that I don't like to write when I'm writing about what I like or know about. It's that I *know* the paper will come back covered with put-downs for all my mistakes in spelling, grammar, and all the rest. It's so discouraging. I just sit in class and count the number of times he contradicts himself or puts somebody else down. He just seems to have to control *everything* and *everybody* in the class. I've heard his wife is a real bitch, though. Makes him jump every time she says 'frog.' Wonder what they are like in bed? I just can't imagine! I can't believe they ever do it!"

Mr. Wordsworthless seems to be a typical professional teacher-controller. If there is any spontaneity in his students when he gets them, they are likely to have much less after he gets through. He thinks he is teaching English literature and correct expression. But what most students learn—if Holly is a typical example—is how rigid, insecure, and cold he is. He touches only with a hand of ice or tongue of acid. He is afraid to get close or be involved at any level. Most of his energy goes to maintain the impenetrability of his psychological armor, and his body, voice, and gestures express this rigidity as well. His encounters with students are always oblique. He never lets "those young punks" face him head-on. Therefore he never levels with them, and he doesn't get their message when they level with him. He invariably mistakes such student expressions for impudence and lack of respect. "Don't you realize I am your teacher?" he thinks, even if he doesn't say it out loud.

Holly can't relate to him, nor he to her. They never really encounter each other. His touch is so completely one of put-down that she must respond with rejection as a defense to her ego. She thinks of him as a *thing*, a tool that puts her down and suppresses her. She would like to *get at* his humanity, and her question at the end is significant. She is saying, "Is he really like me?" She would like to have him be human. But his armor is so completely covering that she cannot even imagine how he could be human. Small wonder *his* lesson is completely lost on her.

So this is one of the kinds of experiences that goes on in school and that is supposed to be educative. But there are others at a "higher" level. Let us listen in on a conversation in the counselor's office of a large high school.

"Hello, David. Come in and sit down. I guess you are here to get your schedule set up for next semester."

"Yes, Mrs. Wilson, I hope I can get a better one than this semester. I seem to get all the things I don't like and don't want."

"Well, what would you like to take next semester?"

"I would like electronics, musical composition, modern poetry, and psychology. You see I want to be a songwriter and musician. I play the guitar now and I figure it would be a good deal if I knew how to compose and arrange my own songs and write my own lyrics. That's why I want musical composition and poetry. I need psychology because I want to write about people and emotions. And electronics—well, it doesn't do any harm to know how to fix my sound system and add to it when I can afford to make it better."

"That sounds very sensible, David. But I am afraid we will have to make some modifications in your choices. In the first place, musical composition and modern poetry are senior subjects, and you are only a junior. Also you have to take beginning harmony before composition. Perhaps you would like to take that now. Next year you could take the composition. For your literature, you could take British poetry and save modern poetry for next year too.

"Of course you know you need to take a laboratory science. I would recommend biology or chemistry. And physical education is required every year in high school too. That makes four subjects with your music and poetry and you can only take five. Which will it be, electronics or psychology? Electronics is only given on Monday and Wednesday afternoons, and that's when your science labs are scheduled so I guess it will have to be psychology."

"Now let's see what that gives you, David. Psychology, British poetry, chemistry, physical education, and beginning harmony. How's that for a schedule? Next year you will be a senior and *all* subjects will be open to you then. Do you have any questions?"

"Yes, Mrs. Wilson, do you know where the Marine Recruiting Office is?"

Do we need to say what David is learning here? Mrs. Wilson might say, "It really isn't my fault. The regulations, the straitjacket, the blind inhumanity, and the inefficiency of the schedule are not mine!" She may feel she is only a cat's paw who does the work of disenchanting and squelching the spontaneity of the youth of today. She has done it for so long that she has taken on the toxic smell of "the monster." Its sulfureous breath hardly phases her any more. In fact her breath has become so acid over the years that it blends right in.

Let us look at this situation more carefully, however. Mrs. Wilson is perhaps one of the few people in the system who might exert a nourishing effect. It is she who is (or should be) trained in the sensitivities and skills of dealing with adolescents. It is she who could bend—if not crack a little—the rigidity of the system. She could, if she chose—and were even a wee bit brave—protect and defend David, and not the monster. But she cops out and prefers to do her thing with the "priests" behind the altar, instead of being a public champion of the heretofore defenseless students who need so very much her heart and her know-how. Yes, David, and his fellows *have been* defenseless. But as they drop out and are forced, by situations such as the one described above, to defend themselves, they will become armored too—like Mr. Words-worthless. They will lose all their sensitive realism and ingenuous honesty. They will either join the "monster" and become one of "them," or they will form their own rebellious group and defend by massive resistance. In either case the goal of self-actualizing development is lost. And the touching which could open doors and melt armor has been replaced by the hard and cold tools of control and dehumanization.

But this isn't all that is learned. Here are some bits of conversations that could be heard at various places in our schools of today.

Place: Bayside Elementary School

"I want all of you elementary teachers to be sure you give the full quota of physical education each day. If it is too cold and rainy, you will each take turns having P.E. in the cafeteria."

"But, Mr. Hardy, I have a student who badly needs to work on his reading. He is just catching on to word-attack skills. If he could just use one or two extra half hours a week he might. . ."

"I'm sorry, Mrs. Merrill, that won't do. The State Education Code says we must have our half hour of P.E. each day and if we must, we will."

"Could I stay after school with him then? He would be tired, but he is very eager to learn and he has been behind for so long it would be a real boost to his ego to learn to read well."

"You know he rides the bus, and the busses leave promptly at 2:30. If you want to drive him home—perhaps. But he lives a good half hour away from the school. I wouldn't advise that. You don't know what his parents might think!"

Place: Assistant Principal's Office, Bay City High School

"Well, John, here you are again. I don't know what I'm going to do with you. Do you know this makes twenty-five referrals this semester—and most of them from Miss Williams! I thought we agreed that you would cause no more trouble in her class!"

"I haven't caused her any trouble Mr. Johnson. I haven't been there very much, and when I am there I usually sleep. She makes me very tired."

"John, do you know what you are saying? The State Code says you *must* go to school, and going to school means going to the classes we schedule you in. You have been regularly truant for over two months now. And as to your sleeping, you owe it to your teacher to be respectful."

"Well, Miss Williams always tells me how fat I am and wants me to be nice and thin and alert. But how can I be? My mother and father are fighting all night so I get very little sleep. My only meals are here at school—at least until I get home again. I slop up cokes and candy bars all day here. I really don't like them, but that's all you have until lunch, and they do keep me going, at least, and give me a lift. When I cut class, I can go into town and get a bowl of hot soup, a fresh sandwich, and an apple. I can't get food like that here at *any* time! All you have are stale packaged sandwiches and some kind of very salty stew or spaghetti."

"Well, John, we can't cater to your dietary fads or be involved in your home problems. Just what do you propose to do? You can't go on like this!"

"I propose to drop my algebra class with Miss Williams!"

And what would you take in place of it? You can't start another class now! You have to take five subjects, or you won't graduate!"

"I don't want to graduate. I just want out. I want to live my life now—not when I am too old to appreciate it!"

"But how will you earn a living? You need a high school education to get a job. When I was your age . . . " (The principal is brought back from his reverie into the past by the soft closing of the door. The seat in front of him is strangely vacant!)

Place: John T. Thurstone High School

"Lucy, your dress and appearance in my class are absolutely inexcusable. I cannot tolerate it any longer and the school has a rule against it. You must wear longer dresses. And you have to wear shoes of some kind not just sandals. Your feet are just filthy! I don't see how you can stand to let other people see you that way."

"Mr. Jackson, most people think I'm pretty. They say they like to look at me. Don't you like to look at me? I notice you look at me often when I am in your class. And tight shoes hurt my feet!"

"What I look at is *my* business, and I consider your remark another one of your signs of disrespect and impudence. If you don't show me more respect, I shall have to lower your grade, and it's not too high right now. Furthermore feet should be covered whether they hurt or not!"

"But Mr. Jackson I can't seem to please you. My dress is too high and my grade is too low. And really they're my feet and they have to last me a long time. I want them in good condition when I'm as advanced in years as you are!"

"That does it! Down to a D! I hope you know what this means. You are no longer eligible to be a candidate for Homecoming Queen!"

These conversations are again an indication of what is learned in our schools today. Some of the basic lessons students learn are: "they" badly need to control me; "they" enjoy punishing me; "they" want me to postpone living till tomorrow, even if tomorrow never comes.

But the teachers, the counselors, the administrators, and the boards of education do not know this! They do not know that it makes very little difference what is *taught*. What is important is what is learned! And the judges of this learning *are not* those who make standardized performance tests. The judges are the students themselves. We must ask the students if we want to know what is learned. And we must ask in such a way that the *real* learnings can come out. We must let students freely respond to questions such as "How do you feel about what goes on in your school? What are your reactions to your classes? How would you change your school if you could?" These questions must be answered in such a way that threat of punishment is reduced to a minimum. In some cases the approach might better be, "Would you like to talk about school? Feel free to say whatever is in your head." Whatever the approach—and one who is genuinely concerned can

122

certainly find an effective one—the result must come freely from the students. When will the "priests" and "temple prostitutes" dare to ask them?

"But what can we do about all this? We have had a school system like this for many years. We can't change it over night. Besides I feel these young people *need* control. Who knows what they would do without it!"

Yes, you are right we have had a school system like this for over a hundred years. We designed our elementary school only to teach students to read the Bible. We copied our high school from Prussia, where the secondary school was used to train officers in the Prussian military system. What can we do? Well, if we want schools to be what school really means, we can at least stop what we are doing now!

"What do you mean stop what we are doing? Have no school at all? And what does school really mean?"

"Well, school comes from a Greek word meaning a resting place, a place of leisure. It is a place away from the troubles and turmoil of everyday life. Does it not seem reasonable from this idea and from what we know of Greek schools of Plato's and Aristotle's time that in such a school one would take the time to get together with one's self and to become whole, healthy, and holy, as we said many times in chapter 9? If so, the school would be much like a temple—a place set apart and consecrated for holiness—for God's work. God's work might be mending splits, as we discussed in chapter 10. Or God's work might be wrestling and getting in touch, as we discussed in chapter 11. In any event, God's work could not be controlling or squelching creativity and spontaneity. To do these things would cause guilt and would also cause a split in the person. When I am controlled, I resent the controller, and if I cannot express my resentment due to the superior power of the controller, I tend to hate myself for not striking out. Hence I develop in me a topdog, who controls me, and an underdog, who is controlled. And I am split, unhealthy, and unholy.

"If holiness, health, and leisure is what school really means and what we want it to mean, then we had better stop almost everything we are doing *now*. It couldn't be worse! We will then need to rebuild and redesign our schools so that they may be "holy" places where all sorts of meaningful encounters can take place with our selves, with the others with whom we live, and with the God who is within us. We will need to reinstitute the idea and necessity of touching. We will need to reinstitute the idea of emotional involvement in school. We will need to bring out the "temple prostitutes" (those mistresses of involvement and holiness) from behind the "altar." We will need to have teachers, administrators, and counselors share their humanness, their hearts, and their feelings with students. We will need to make the process public, not hidden. We will particularly need to be sure that what goes on in the "high places"—the boards of education, the administration, the counseling center—does not pollute or dilute the holiness below. We will need to make schools places of leisure, of softness, of creativity. And we will need to make the only form of control that control which flows from within—from the kingdom of heaven which is within us all!

14

The Reasonableness
of
Irrationality

In our previous chapter on schools, we never mentioned the medieval goal of schools and universities alike: to defend the faith against all heresies and unbelievers. To conduct this kind of defense meant to carry on a kind of court trial. The defender of the faith was put on the stand, and he was then bombarded with questions (this, of course, after he had made a preliminary statement of what were the essential tenets of the faith).

The defense of the faith would be the defense of reason. A particular question would be analyzed by the defender to reveal its various shades of meaning. Each meaning would then be refuted—shot down, as it were. All of this—the analysis and the refutation—must follow according to the canons of formal logic which would be largely according to Aristotle. There would be learned "doctors" in the "courtroom" who would judge whether the defense had been adequate or not. In case the defense were judged inadequate, another defender might take the stand. Were the attack so penetrating that it could not be repulsed, then and only then might the articles of faith be modified.

Today we use this "method of reason" in many areas of life. We have built our court system on it, and often the life or liberty of a citizen may depend on its effective use. We use it to some extent in the conduct of scientific research. And we even have the vestigial remains of it in some of our churches and religious organizations.

Let us see what goes on when we use this method. In the first place, the method of reason says, "I am God. I am impersonal, objective, unemotional. I am the way to the Truth. There may be other doors to the Truth but they can only be warranted by me! If you deny me, you deny the Truth. No man comes to the Truth except through me!"

For those who subscribe to this idea, reason *must* be part and parcel of the schools. It must be the goal of the schools to train students to be reasonable, and the schools must, themselves, be organized in a reasonable way. This means that schools and their personnel must be impersonal and unemotional. They must deal with people as though they had minds and no feelings. If and when feelings and emotions do arise, they must be squelched, or at least ruled out of order in classrooms and other places where "learning" is supposed to take place. One would never dream of trying to develop more feelings and richer emotions in school. Furthermore, schools must also train students to be equally reasonable—hence impersonal and unemotional—in conducting the important aspects of life.

Reason, then, forms a wall, or a curtain, which drops whenever emotion or irrationality enters the scene. All we need to say is, "Why don't you be reasonable?" And we have our opponent licked. Any procedure or technique can be killed if it can be labeled unreasonable. Were a teacher or administrator "proven" to be repeatedly unreasonable, he might lose his job almost as easily as if he were morally corrupt or incompetent in other ways. No elected official could ever succeed in getting into office were he to run on a platform of unreasonableness or irrationality even though, when elected, he might operate with an almost complete lack of reason. He must promise reason even though he knows he cannot or will not deliver it.

"What are you saying then? Do you want people and schools and officials to be irrational? Don't you feel truth is important? Isn't it necessary to use reason to get at truth? And don't we want our lives based on truth and not falsity?"

These are all very good questions. But they avoid a very important point. What kind of a person do you want to be? Do you want to be together and whole? Do you want to be able to take responsibility for what you do and feel? Do you want to get to know yourself more and more fully? Do you want to be able to flow with your experiences? Will you risk losing control and being wrong in order to achieve these things?

If you answer "yes" to these questions then you must realize that reason, truth, and logical consistency may have to take a back seat. Reason is a method of external control. It does not flow from within. No one was ever born reasonable. The canons of logic and reason were derived by somebody else at some other time. Even Aristotle was necessarily controlled *externally* by the logic he developed *then* at some other time. In order to live together and responsibly, I must focus my attention *now* on what is here *now* within me and around me. My controls must flow out of *me*. I must be new each day, not recreated out of nothing that ever was, but newly organized and newly flowing in a new way. I am committed to no external canons of behavior which came out of a *then*. I am committed to me and all that is mine—within and without. These things *now* are my controls. I do not need to marshall them into action. They naturally come into operation as I need them. In fact, they are really me. So I had better say, "*I* come into being *now* as I need me. I create and recreate me as I flow along. This is my existence and this is all right, even though I may encounter pain and displeasure sometimes in the process!"

Reason, then, insofar as it is a form of external control, is an opponent of the *now*. It is essentially a *then* thing and always calls us to look at and focus on a *then*. Reason takes us apart in that it makes of us a controlling part and an undergoing part. Reason also takes ideas apart. It analyzes them. A faith that has been reasoned is a collection of parts which may seem to be consistent. However they have no real unity or holiness since they were *put* together as parts. They were not *born* together as a whole. One cannot create, or give birth to, a person or any living organism by assembling a collection of parts. To be alive means to be born together. Hence reason is life- and health-destroying. Furthermore a "reasoned faith" is itself a contradiction and an impossibility. Once a faith has been reasoned—put together out of parts—it is only a mockery of faith. It cannot be believed if belief means to take as a whole without any reservation. It cannot be holy, since it is not whole. Furthermore to take a deeply held belief and reasonably analyze it is to kill it. Hence reason and faith, reason and life, reason and now, are pairs which are necessarily in opposition. The "court of reason" and the defense by reason are idea-defeating and person-destroying. After I have been defended, I may be dead in terms of my emotional involvement. After an idea is defended, it has lost all of its dynamic power to capture the hearts of men. Persons and ideas that live and flow and touch our lives are, then, unreasoned. But they are beautifully together and holy.

"Well it all sounds very confusing to me! I always thought that the way to have a strong belief was to put it together carefully. Then it would have less chance of having inconsistencies in it. Hence there would be less chance that doubt would creep into the mind of one who believed it. Is this not so?"

I am not sure if this is so or not. But I don't believe it. As I have said, a reasoned belief is a constructed belief, a dead belief. It was not born and embraced whole. Or it is a live belief which was killed by analysis and is now no longer an object for belief as a whole. As far as consistency goes, this, of course, is determined by reasonable analysis. But whose categories for analysis do we use? You may say I do not arise consistently in the morning because I never get up at the same time. However I may say I am consistent because I always get out of bed on the same side, and I am always in the same bad mood with the same bad breath. Consistency depends on the choice of the analyzer.

Furthermore the strength of my belief has really nothing to do with consistency. I believe that which I cannot and do not want to doubt. In a sense the belief strikes me as a whole, captures my attention, and I fall in love with it. My belief, and the process of believing, are personal and very involving things. And I do not seek to find faults or inconsistencies in them. I accept them fully and completely as they are, and I operate with them in that way. Were I even to look *seriously* for inconsistencies in my belief and thus to analyze it, I am sure I would kill it and therefore would no longer believe it, no matter how many consistencies or inconsistencies I found. Even when I want to analyze it, I have probably already "fallen out of love" with it and no longer believe it. Perhaps it would help to give an example of how the attempt to subject a belief to reasonable analysis is self-defeating.

Suppose I believe that a particular diet will alleviate a particular organic malfunctioning. I have this on the word of my doctor. Suppose my friend believes that such a disability can only be alleviated by the use of drugs and medicines. He, in fact, has this disability and is in the process of using drugs and medicines to alleviate it. The medicines are having very little positive effect. However the malady is no worse than it was. He is understandably not pleased with this state of affairs.

I suggest that he stop his medication and try my diet, and that he not use both as it is my belief, and my doctor's, that one would interfere with the other. He is reluctant to do this and asks for some proof or evidence that my diet will do the job. I have no evidence to give other than my own belief and the word of my doctor. I ask what benefit would the evidence serve. He says this would make the chances of success more *probable*, and it would then be more *reasonable* for him to take the chance. I reply that statistical probability will never cure anyone. Were he to try the diet and not believe in it, it may well have no beneficial effect at all. His reasonable "scientific tentativeness" may be the block to his being cured.

I next ask, how would he know whether my evidence—if I had any— were valid or not? What would be the canons on which he would determine this validity? He does not know. But he admits that whatever they would be, they must be a matter of choice. Hence the supposed validity of the evidence, his willingness to accept it, his willingness to accept my belief, and his further willingness to try the diet are a matter of his choice. They are all a matter of belief—a total belief, a total committment—that this diet, in fact, will do the job.

"But isn't that a hell of a gamble? What if he dies from this diet, and the giving up of his medication?"

Who knows what one dies from? But you are quite right. He may die and will ultimately die for sure. And, of course, any committment is a gamble. But one can only flow if one will let go—let go of caution, let go of control, let go of reason, let go of the demands for evidence and proof before acting. Whether he does any of these things is a matter of choice. He can just as well choose to believe as to be cautious. But in believing, and being unreasonable, he is acting as a whole and accepting the belief as a whole too. This believing, in itself, produces an effect in him—one which puts him more securely together than he was before.

"But irrationality is much more than being unreasonable. You have said in the title of this chapter that irrationality is reasonable. What do you mean?"

Yes, irrationality is the courting of unreasonableness. I may be unreasonable because I have made a mistake or a slip in my thoughts or actions. But irrationality means to avoid *intentionally* being reasonable, to throw consistency aside, to be, in a sense, mad or insane.

My title is another paradox like the one in chapter 5 on control. If I want to lose control and come together, it is "reasonable" (in the sense of being sensible and productive of my desired result) to be irrational. If I want to lose control, I'd better jolly well lose it and lose it *completely*. I'd better also not even plan, reasonably, to achieve this result. I just know that by being irrational I will flow. And in the flow will come many desirable results, although I do not know specifically what these results will be before they occur. It is, therefore, reasonable for me to be irrational if I want to be reborn and want to flow. It is in being irrational that newness emerges. And the newness that emerges is me in a new form.

"How can I be irrational? I have trained myself to be reasonable and valid and right for so long. I don't know where to start."

There are many gates to the irrational. Some of these are like those mentioned in chapter 11, the getting in touch with myself and the wrestling with God. The fantasies are also a good way to reach the irrational, particularly if you can leave the real world of your life and fantasize an existence that violates all "natural" laws.

An additional "gate" is speaking in tongues—the repeating of nonsense words and sounds in a metrical or semi-metrical way. You can do this by yourself or with others. But it is usually easier to learn in a group. One person starts to spout words in a meaningless way, attempting to violate any pattern of rhyme or idea. An example might be:

Free and flowing, flowing free. I am a man and you are a tree, but trees have arms and legs and ears and leaves and I never like yesses or tresses or torn dirty dresses. Or boxes of torn grass on fire at last in a house at the bottom of the sea, hi de hi ho de hee hum hum arf, irf, ink, can, sun, shit. This is really senseless why don't you split.

This needs to be done rapidly and then the next person takes over. If there is a hesitation, someone else picks it up. Moments of silence are to be avoided. This procedure can go on for almost any length of time. As a group or a person gets used to being verbally irrational and can throw off controls, the lengths of time of the irrational trip grows. Ultimately there may be no limit to how long it will go. After such an experience, feelings can be shared. Some persons are usually greatly released. Others become uptight. Describing these feelings in detail will add a great deal to the experience.

As one goes into the irrational, you can look at your typical day and squeeze a bit of the reasonableness out of it. Can you afford to forget something important? Can you be late for an appointment? Can you not do some act in your usual daily routine—such as shave, comb your hair, or eat on time? Can you be irresponsible in carrying out the expectations of others and of yourself? If so this may be another gate to the irrational.

"But what will I become if I do this. What will people think of me? I would be afraid my life would fall apart, have no predictability. I might lose my job, my wife, my friends!"

You *will* be different. But can you afford to gamble a little? Think how much of your life is now ordered, scheduled, routined. Could you not afford a bit of irresponsibility, of unpredictable irrationality? If so, you can learn *how* to lose control. When you do that, you can learn to control by flow, as the rain does. And you can be easier and more together in your internal control. Seen in this way, irrationality becomes an instrument for self-actualization, a way of losing the tensions and stresses which pull us apart!

131

15

Expectations

Life or Death
of
Relationships?

I am not in this world to live up to your expectations,
And you are not in this world to live up to mine.

Question: But under these circumstances, what do *you* expect
me to do?
Answer: Under these circumstances, what do *you* expect *you*
to do?

We are brought up to be continually expecting. We expect mail to
be delivered at a particular time. We expect bills to arrive on the first
day of each month. We expect a child to be born after nine months of
pregnancy. We expect menstrual flow after twenty-eight days in
between. We expect dinner to be at a certain hour. We expect to be
paid on pay day. We expect faithfulness from our lovers, husbands,
and wives. We expect obedience from our dogs and our children. We
expect consideration, kindness, consistency, reciprocity, justice, and on
some occasions we expect the opposite of these qualities. We expect
festivity at parties and on holidays. We expect cards and gifts on
certain special occasions; we expect thanks and gratitude on others.
And after certain events, we expect to have headaches, hangovers,
and a general feeling of negativity. All these things we are pro-
grammed to expect and when they do not materialize, we are at least
surprised if not disappointed. Our disappointments often come as a

result of unrealized expectations. These cause our greatest feelings of depression.

"But I get my kicks out of life by what I look forward to. As a kid I looked forward to Christmas, birthdays, and vacations. I looked forward to my dad coming home from work. And I looked forward to going on leave when I was in the Armed Services. I look forward to being greeted with a kiss and a hug when I see my girl friend. I look forward to a well-mixed drink and a good meal when I go to my favorite restaurant. I look forward to an interesting evening of theater when I go to a play by my favorite author, acted by one of my favorite actresses. I look forward to warm weather in spring and summer. And I look forward to the changing colors and crispness in the air in autumn. All of these are expectations. They are the very spice of my life. Were I to be without these, I would feel life had lost its sparkle."

Yes, of course, you are quite right. We *do* expect. We can hardly stop expecting. In fact it is by these expectations that life develops some of its flow, some of its consistency. So it is at least questionable whether we would want to do away with our expectations, even if we could do so. When an expectation comes true it gives us very little trouble. In fact we are usually overjoyed. We are pleased with the result itself. We are also pleased at the way the result worked out. For example, when I buy you a gift, I am pleased *in anticipation* of your response. When you *do* respond with pleasure, I am doubly pleased. But what if you don't like it? What if my expectation does not materialize? That's when the situation gets difficult. That's when I am likely to go into one of those tornadoes of depression which was described in chapter 7. The problem, then, is not with the expectation. The problem is that I expect *you* to work out or fulfill my expectation. I want to use my expectation as a kind of standard or control of your behavior. If you act in accordance with my expectation, you and your behavior are good, right, acceptable. If you do not act in accordance with my expectations, you and your behavior are bad, wrong, unacceptable.

Of course I may also turn this whole thing on myself as well. If *I* do not act so as to fulfill my expectations for myself, I am bad and my behavior is unacceptable. If *I* do act so as to fulfill my expectations for myself, I am good and my behavior is acceptable. But there is a great difference here. I can, if I want to accept this fact, be responsible for my own behavior. If so I can work toward a greater fulfillment of my own expectations for my self. But I am not, nor can I very effectively try to be, responsible for *your* behavior. Therefore I can hardly work toward *your* fulfilling *my* expectations for you and your behavior. My dividends from my expectations come, then, from my working on my own behavior, not on being concerned with your behavior. Perhaps this will be clearer in the following example.

I am a tired husband coming home from my office. I have had a long hard day full of many frustrations and a few outstanding successes. The traffic on the freeway was heavy, and I am very tense as I get out of my car and come up the steps to the front door of my house.

You are my wife. I expect you to have dinner ready or at least in preparation. I expect the house will be relatively in order, as this is the day the cleaning woman usually comes in to clean.

I open the front door and call your name. No one is at home. I go into the bedroom and things are obviously not in order. The bed is not made. Clothes are not picked up. The same is true of the kitchen and the rest of the house. Dishes are unwashed in the sink. Newspapers are strewn around the living room. Pieces of half-opened mail are on the dining room table. I wonder, and as I wonder my expectations fall, and I become tense with a mixture of disappointment and growing resentment.

I go to the refrigerator to mix myself a drink to pick me up a bit. No ice! I decide I will have scotch and tap water, or better yet, scotch straight in a brandy breather. I sit sipping my drink, not so slowly, and looking blankly at the fireplace.

After my second or third scotch, I hear your car pull up, and I hear you hurrying up the steps toward the front door. I just sit there and wait for you to come in. When you do come in, I just look at you as if to say, "Well *there* you are!"

You are obviously hurried and flustered. You go to the kitchen to put down your arm-load of packages. I help you a bit but not too skillfully. When you have stored everything, you make a hurried trip to the bathroom. We have hardly exchanged any words. I go back to my sipping, looking at the fireplace, and resenting. It is obvious to both of us that the situation is charged. Neither of us knows how to escape it, how to escape *us*.

You return in a few minutes and tell me that at 10:00 A.M. you got a hurried call from your good friend, Jenny, that her husband had left her. You just *had* to go to her and you have been with her all day. She was nearly hysterical. Finally you partially calmed her and just had time to stop by the supermarket on the way home to get something for dinner. "I'm sorry it took so long, dear, but what else could I do?" You say, "Dinner will only take a half-hour or so. I guess Mary didn't come to clean, did she?"

I am filled with unfulfilled expectations. How can I handle them? There are at least two ways. Let us listen to them. One might go like this:

> You're sorry *it* took so long? You mean you're sorry *you* took so long with that sad-assed bitch, Jenny. No *wonder* her husband left her! I don't see why he waited so long!
>
> "What could you do? You could look at your God-damned watch and think of your *own* husband. That's what you could do! This house is a mess! I'm hungry! Or I *was* hungry. And to make matters worse, there's not even *one cube* of ice in the refrigerator! I don't know why I even bothered to come home. I could just as well have eaten dinner downtown!

We need not go into your response. Whether it is tears, an equal retort, a stony silence, or a speedy departure by way of the nearest door, we can be sure that any enjoyment is gone for the rest of the evening— and perhaps even longer.

A second way I could handle the situation might be like this:

> "Well, Audrey, I was so uptight from my hectic day and the traffic on the freeway that I just came home and proceeded to dissolve my tensions in scotch. Now I'm so hungry I don't want to wait. Why don't we go down to La Casita Hermosa and have dinner there? They have good hot food and it's quick. Besides those mariachis there will help to take my mind off my troubles. Can the food you bought wait until another day?"

What I have said is all very true. But I did *not* mention my expectations for you and for the condition of our home. I *am* uptight at waiting for you and I *am* uptight about the mess too. But need I mention this? If you are at all perceptive, you know this anyway. You even knew it *before* you got home. And you may have more than a small pang of guilt about this. Were I to hit you with my expectations, no matter how gently, the result could hardly be positive. I, of course, might say to myself, "I just *have* to let her know *exactly* how I feel. It's the only honest thing to do. She has a right to know how I feel *fully*. And I have a right to express myself *fully*. It's the only way we can build a firm and dependable relationship." But I wouldn't *really* believe this *within* myself. Were I to unload more fully and mention the sore spots, it would probably be because I wanted to upset myself and create an uproar, as was described in chapter 3. This is, of course, okay if that's what I want. But if I want to enjoy the evening and my life with Audrey I need to hold back from the tendency of belaboring the obvious, particularly when it hits a sore spot.

The key to handling my unfulfilled expectations, then, is to decide whether I want to have free, full expression of my feelings whatever the cost, or whether I want to deal with my expectations so as to build deeper and richer patterns of involvement with those I am closely associated with. Or do I want some combination of the two? If I demand free and full expression *at all costs*, the cost will probably be that I will have few, if any close relationships—and that is all right, if it is really what I want. In this case I simply uncork and lay my shit on the line, letting it fall wherever it may.

But let us assume that I do want to build deeper and richer relationships, and yet I seem to regularly "blow it" by uncorking my unfulfilled expectations of my associates at the wrong time and in the wrong ways. What can I do?

Well, the first thing I can do when I get home is to sit down and take stock of my expectations and the feelings and emotions they are creating—really *I* am creating—*in me*. If no one is home, it is easier. If someone is home, I had best go off by myself to take a mini-wilderness trip for at least twenty minutes or a half an hour. During this time alone, I should try fully to get in touch with all my expectations and my feelings about them. It might go like this:

"God damn! She isn't here yet! Wonder where she is this time? And look at this house! It's a mess, a shitty mess. I almost wish I never owned it! Wonder how long I'll have to wait? I'm starved and pissed off and tired and tense. What the hell does she expect me to do now? She could at least leave a message! I'd like to throw or hit something. My hands and arms are all tense, and the feeling is moving up to my shoulders and neck! This is a fucked up mess! I can't just sit here. I have to walk around at least. My breathing is shallow. I feel empty and cold inside my stomach and chest. I better go out on the porch and take a breath. No, I need to yell and open up my neck, throat, and chest. I'll go in the bedroom and lock the door. I can let it out there. I'll yell and scream and pound on the bed with both my hands!"

(I do this and after I am exhausted and somewhat relieved, I go out on the porch where the air is calm and refreshing.)

"I feel better now. I am still pissed off but not so much at her as at me. *I* fucked up my day at the office. Went in too tense, too compulsive about signing up that new contract. Traffic was bad, but nothing unusual. Why am I so upset when she isn't home? That really bugs me! She *always* has our best interests at heart. When she isn't here, it's usually for a good reason. Am I suspicious? If so, of what? I really don't know, or I don't let myself know. I must be making all kinds of weird fantasies about her. Is this all I can think of? I need more relaxing things to do with my head and body. I'll just sit here and look out over the hills and let my eyes wonder. That's good! Every time my eyes hit that purple clump of flowers over there I get a little shiver of delight in my spine! I need to do this more often. How peaceful and calm and cool it is out here! First shadows of evening are a bluish, purplish, black. It cools me. I feel waves of coolness coming over and through my body. Each cool wave is followed by a warmer one. I really feel alive. I still tingle all over from the pounding, but it's good!

"Ah! Here she is! I'll tell her about the office and my fuck up. I'll tell her how relieved I feel now. I'll just let her day come out in whatever way she wants it to come. I know if she is this late that she feels bad about it too. Wonder if she will want to go out to dinner? It's okay either way with me. The main thing is that *I* feel much more together now!"

We see here that the speaker has turned his attention directly to his own behavior and to his own expectations for himself. He quickly leaves his expectations for his wife. When he does this, he is in an area over which he can exert some control and expect to produce some results. He is not in the world to fulfill her expectations, nor she his. But is he in the world to fulfill *his* expectations for himself?

This last question is a most crucial one, and the answer is most controversial. Let us again listen to two ways of dealing with this question:

> "When I left the Service, I was already enrolled in college. I applied months before I was separated. I have a nice apartment in the student housing where my wife and I live with our two children. I am well along the way toward my degree. I only have twenty more units to take and I will be through. I expect to get a good job in some space industry when I am graduated. I have already been interviewed by three corporations. Prospects look very good. Seems as though it would be a good time to start on our third child so the age difference between them won't be too great. I am not sure where we will live, but there is a good chance it will be the West Coast. I'm looking forward to getting our new home started!"

This might be called the *ladder approach* to handling expectations. One expectation leads to another above it or beyond it. The goal is to get above or beyond. It is always out there. Here and now is always for the purpose and benefit of the goal out there. The speaker is accomplishing what he wants, or says he wants. He has certain expectations for himself and is *driving* himself to achieve them. Among these expectations are job, children, home. One would expect that it would be quite tragic if something blocked or interfered with the progress up the ladder. What if the space industries suffer a serious cutback in their operations? What if the speaker's health was seriously impaired? What if an expensive operation made it necessary for him to get a full-time job immediately? This would be like the rungs falling out of the ladder in his immediate vicinity. He would have no access to his expected goal. He would have no clear way to his personal expectations.

Also what if he were hired in the job of his choice and it were necessary for him to leave his family behind for a considerable length of time? Or suppose the best job offer were in a location where schools and living conditions were intolerable in the opinion of his wife? These considerations would be seen as blocks to going up the ladder. Therefore the ladder approach to dealing with his expectations might leave him at a loss. The ladder leaves one with no choices but up or down, and no one wants to go down!

Here is a second way of dealing with the problem of fulfilling personal expectations:

> "I have been through three years in the Armed Services and two years in college, and I am confused. When I got out, I thought I knew what I wanted—a good time and a good job. That meant money to me—M-O-N-E-Y!"

> "Now as I go along in college and in life, I don't know where I want to go. I have been married once and that didn't work out. Thank God, no children! I started out in college learning about business and finance. But I'm getting fed up with that stuff. Lately I've been turned on to people, and music, and all the interesting things that go with these two. I'm learning to play the piano, and I am writing songs—yes, music and lyrics! I get a real kick out of this, too! Also I'm getting to know myself. I like to lie back on the beach and listen to the waves. Or go out in the desert at night and look up at the stars. The world has developed so much glamour and fascination for me. It is like I have fallen in love with life. A few years ago I was in Viet Nam busy wiping out other lives when on duty, and deadening myself when off. Now I am in love with me and what goes on every day. Of course I have my bummers. But getting out of the Service and out of that money hangup were the best things I ever did. I don't know where I am going. I don't know where I will be next week or next year. But I do know where I am—and I like it!"

This speaker is not on a ladder although he evidently was at one time. He seems to have no clear-cut expectations for himself—at least none which are time-bound. He wants to write music, to know himself and other people. He wants to expand into nature. But he has no schedule, no program, no clear-cut direction. We might call his way of handling expectations the *wanderer's method*. There is always something to put a glint in the eye and an extra beat in the heart. But it is never to be found in any consistent direction or place. He wanders and floats in life's stream and in the process, expectations develop, pass by, and change at a moment's notice. One expectation may fade as a

139

much more beautiful one is developing. They are achieved and realized because they are *not* forced or controlled. They just arrive and are taken advantage of when the time is ripe.

"But what of all the expectations I have for myself that do not ever come to maturity? What of all the things I want to do and achieve that seem to pass me by? Can't I somehow press myself into line to achieve and conquer them by the exercise of great effort?"

Well I guess you haven't gotten the message. If you *did* press yourself onto the "ladder of success," you might very well lose what you really want. In the pressing, the controlling, in the muscling of ego, you will lose yourself—that self that lives and breathes and grows spontaneously. When you try to press yourself, you make *two* selves, a topdog and an underdog, as we saw in chapter 10. And you can no more be responsible for that underdog's behavior than you can the behavior of someone else. You must get together. Let top and under have it out and face themselves. If you do, you can, in a noncompulsive way, deal with what happens—what naturally and spontaneously occurs in the flow of your experiences. Now you will be one. You will have atoned ("at oned") for your compulsive pressure. You will be in touch with what is inside you. And you, *now*, can face yourself, your inner self, your feelings, your emotions, and your expectations. When you do this, when you go to your wilderness to wrestle, you will come out knowing who you are much more deeply. Now expectations will come to maturity naturally, without superimposed ego pressure. Now expectations will flow through you. Some of them you will achieve, others you will discard, and still others you may never reach. But you will be joyous in the fulfillment of those you do achieve *now* and will not regret the could-have-beens!

So expectations cannot be avoided and should not be. I will watch to see whether my expectations for you materialize. Whether they do or not, I will know you and me better, more fully. For this I am grateful. But I can not *require* you to do *anything*—certainly not anything about fulfilling my expectations.

My expectations for me are another matter. If I am together, they will pass through me and I will learn from them. But if I try to pressure myself, I am dead. And in my place is a divided person who must be mended before my life and my expectations can be full again.

16

After Now
What?

So now is touch time. It is the time when I am alive. Whatever I do now, I do in the fullness of my experience. It may be painful and cause pain. It may be joyous and cause ecstasy. Whatever it is, I will flow with it to the fullest if I do it now.

If I do it now, it becomes a part of me. This is because I *live* only in the now. It is in the now that I build my self. Whatever I do now, becomes a part of me, and as such it must not be denied. To deny a part of me is to kill a bit of me. So I need not apologize or excuse or regret or ask forgiveness for what I do now!

It is only when I act there or then that I need to be forgiven. I have killed a bit of myself. I have lived "out of touch." Therefore I have violated myself and correspondingly have violated you in the same action. This is the greatest wrong, the greatest waste, the greatest violation of humanity. This is the real meaning of exploitation—to live *then*, to deal with you for *then*, to "encounter" you without touching, to make a wall between you and me so we do not touch.

"Now all this is crazy! Do you mean that you take seriously the idea that I should 'Take no thought for the morrow: For the morrow shall take thought for the things of itself'? I have bills to pay, and a family to feed, and a job to plan for. And I have life insurance, car insurance, fire insurance, health insurance, theft insurance, and I don't know how many others. I couldn't sleep at night if I weren't protected against all kinds of then's. I have a hell of a good time in the now when I am on a boat trip, or on a vacation, or on a holiday excursion, or at a really good party. Then I can let my hair down and really live it up! But, my God, I have to come back from those experiences to the *real world*! You wouldn't expect me to live like that every day would you?"

I don't expect you to do anything! I have no expectations for you in this regard. But do you, or could you, want to live every day fully? Or do you just want to walk through all these somber obligations, killing all of your now's with this overconcern for then? You must answer. But be sure you make your answer a *now* answer—a real active choice. Then you need not regret it. You can choose to live or die. And since it is your life and your experience it is perfectly all right whatever you do!

You can choose to escape life and not be aware of yourself or of others, and that's all right. You can choose to build your awareness and to continually take in more of yourself and of what is around you, and that's all right too! You can choose to control yourself and others, or you can choose to learn how to lose your control and flow with the river of life, and either of these is all right! You can choose to live in the valley of depression, on the peak or the plateau of feelings. You can choose to poison or nourish. You can choose to encounter your two selves or avoid them. You can choose to wrestle and fast in the wilderness or live in the lap of affluent luxury surrounded *always* by your associates, and these are all right! You can choose to go along with the existing school status quo, or you can choose to resist and fight to redesign it, and either of these is all right! You can choose the life of reason and that's all right! Or you can gamble with excursions into irrationality, and that's all right too! You can ride your own crusade, forcing expectations to be fufilled. Or you can let your expectations flow freely. Either of these is all right! In fact, whatever you *choose* as an active, present, aware decision is all right because it is a part of you. You did it, and for you, you are all right! What has been shown in these pages is simply that there are alternatives to the life of there and then. Whether you choose any of them is *up to you!*

"So where does now go? What comes next? I need to see some purpose, some dividends in my life!"

I really can't help you here. Now is essentially purposeless. It leads nowhere. It just *is!* If you live now, you spend all of your experience. You attempt to save nothing for some other time, for a then.

What comes next? One answer is another now. But what it will be like, I do not know. It will be just as unpredictable, just as permanent or evanescent, just as painful or enjoyable as the present one. There *can* always be another now if we choose it. Or we can stop the choice and elect to kill now. Then the next, the inevitable next, is Death. To kill now is to end life. We always have that alternative, and if we choose it and don't just stumble into it, *that's all right!*

My choices—active and conscious—are always all right. My anesthetized mistakes of "good fortunes" are nothing. They are not real experiences and hence are not *me* or even a *part* of me. They are not touches. They are not now! In choosing, I touch. I make a contact in the now. I choose to touch because of the contact, because of the involvement, because of the touch I get back. And so I choose to touch you, and that's all right. Yes, that's all right as long as I realize I can only touch you now!

Appendix

Activities for Producing Touch and Awareness

Throughout this book touch, awareness, and control have been stressed. Control of the right kind is crucial. It can only be developed by one who knows how to touch and who is also aware. Such a person must be aware of what is going on in himself as well as in others. Only if he is in touch with himself, can he adequately interpret the behavior of others. He must know how to touch by skin contact and also by word, look, and gesture.

In several chapters, exercises were suggested which were designed to help develop a heightened awareness, a more effective control, and a more sensitive way of touching. However, there are many more which could be used.

In the attempt to expand this sample of exercises, the following additions are presented. It should be clear that this list is by no means complete. Those who want still others, should consult the list of reading which follows. Furthermore, all of these activities are by no means original with the writer. Some I have developed myself. Some are borrowed directly from others. Some are my variations on another's theme. All have been given the personal flavor and style that work best for me.

In order to make this collection of activities more manageable, they are presented under the following headings: Direct Touching, Fantasies, Verbal Descriptions, and Verbal Dialogues. Most of them are designed to be shared with at least one other person. In some cases they can be carried out alone, but the dividends are greatly increased by sharing wherever possible. Many activities are to be carried out in a group.

Direct Touching

Hand dialogue

Touching hands and feet was mentioned in chapter 9 as a good "safe" way to introduce direct touching to those who have had little experience with this kind of activity. The hand dialogue is another useful technique of a similar kind. The instructions are as follows:

Close your eyes and turn off your thoughts as completely as you can. To help with this, take five deep breaths and pay attention to your breathing and bodily sensations as you do this. Breathe slowly and deeply. I will count with you to help set the pace: in, out, in, out (etc.).

Now put your left hand in front of you, palm up. Touch your left hand softly with your right hand. As you do this, turn your attention to the sensations in your left hand. Try to turn off the sensations in your right hand. Touch all over the palm of your left hand. Move now to the back and fingers of your left hand. In doing this, use the same fingers of your right hand throughout. (Continue this procedure for perhaps three or four minutes.)

Now switch hands. Let your left hand be the toucher and your right hand be touched. Again try to turn off the sensations in your left hand and focus only on those in your right hand. (Continue for three or four minutes.)

Now go back to your left hand again. Touch it with your right, while you pay attention to your *left* hand. While you are doing this, switch your attention—not your hands. That is, pay attention to the sensation in your *right* hand while it is *touching*. Continue touching but switch your attention back to your left hand. Switch again (Three or four switches in attention should be made here.)

145

Now, open your eyes. Look at each of your hands. Pay attention to the kinds of feelings in each of them. Give your left hand a voice and let it say how it feels. Let your right hand answer this voice and also tell how it feels. (Continue this for three or four exchanges.)

Now, what are your feelings and reactions to all of this? It will be important to take note of differences in sensations in the two hands, blocks of feeling, inability to turn off either hand, and the quality of the voices as well as the ideas and feelings expressed by each hand.

Nonverbal vs. verbal touch

This activity is designed to show the differences between three kinds of touching, two nonverbal and one verbal, and to develop skill in each. For the activity, individuals are paired off. The instructions are as follows:

Sit facing your partner, without making any body contact, and look directly at him for a few minutes. Pay attention to what you are feeling (twenty or thirty seconds duration). Now look at him trying to be aware of what *he* is feeling (twenty to thirty seconds). Try to communicate your feelings and thoughts to him using no body contact at all (one to two minutes).

Now close your eyes and reach out your two hands and hold your partners two hands. With your eyes still closed, be aware of your feelings (twenty to thirty seconds). Now turn your attention to your partner trying to be aware of what *he* is feeling (twenty to thirty seconds). Try to communicate your feelings and thoughts to your partner, using *only* your body contact (one to two minutes).

Open your eyes, and use words now to tell your partner what you experienced in the previous activities and what you feel now. Communicate as fully and freely as you can (five to ten minutes).

Now turn off your words and go back to the nonverbal modes of expression. Continue your communication as fully and freely as you can (two to three minutes). Now back to words again and share your reactions and experiences to all of this!

Time should be provided so that all pairs can share their full experiences with the group and interpret what has happened if this seems desired. It will be important to take note of which feelings grow, which feelings diminish, and which feelings stay the same as this exercise progresses.

Lifting and rocking

This is an exercise with great power to sensitize the individual to his own deeper feelings. It also has great unifying power for any group that participates in it. The exercise is performed by the group on one person at a time, but it may be repeated so that each person may have a chance to experience it. The instructions are as follows:

One person is asked to stand and is then surrounded by six or eight of the group who stand close to him. The subject is asked to shut his eyes. He stands for a minute and senses his feelings. He is then asked to let himself go and fall backward. He is caught by the group member nearest him and is gently laid on the floor on his back.

The group members then put their hands under the person and slowly lift him, rocking him back and forth from head to foot as they do so. They lift him to shoulder height and continue to rock him ten or twelve times in this position. Then they gradually lower him, still rocking.

When the person reaches the floor, all the group members "cover him with their hands" by putting both of their hands on his body. They keep their hands so placed for ten or fifteen seconds and gradually remove them. The times for doing the rocking, lowering, and covering will need to be directed by some one person.

This activity often brings out memories of childhood and with it tears and sobbing. If this occurs, it should be encouraged and allowed to run its course while the group members remain in touch (bodily contact) with the person.

In any event the experience is very moving to most persons, and heightens their awareness of many internal feelings. The group also develops a feeling of caring and concern for each other. This is particularly true if each group member is lifted and rocked. Whatever feelings are generated should be shared fully after the exercise is concluded.

Passing the body

This exercise begins like the previous one. Six or eight group members surround one person with arms and hands free. The person puts his arms at his side, closes his eyes, and falls, keeping his body stiff. He is then passed around the circle from person to person. His feet stay still on the floor and he is rolled around the circle as though he were a log. After about five minutes of this, the subject is asked to open his eyes and stand still and look at each one in the circle. Then another person is chosen.

After each group member has had a chance at this, feelings are shared and interpretations are given. This activity, too, has a strong unifying effect on the group.

Breaking out

The group is asked, "Who is uptight and wants to become loose?" The person who volunteers is put in a circle of abut ten to twelve group members. The group members lock arms and form as tight and close a circle as they can around the person.

The person is then told to break out. "The circle is your up-tightness. If you want to lose it, break out!" Group members naturally resist the breakout and it is hoped that a real struggle will ensue. At length the group member gets out or gives up. In any event it is a very releasing exercise both physically and psychologically.

Each member is given a chance to do this and at the end, feelings and reactions are shared. It is well to get rid of glasses and other hard objects in the apparel of each person before starting the activity.

Breaking in

The group is asked, "Who is a loner, or feels he is? Who wants to lose this feeling?" One person is then put *outside* of a circle of ten or twelve group members who reinforce themselves by locking arms.

The person is then told, "Here is the group that excludes you. They represent all those who have kept you out. Now break in!" The person uses all his strength and ingenuity to get in and eventually does so or gives up. After each one has had a chance at this, their experiences are shared fully.

Stretching the limits of touch

Individuals are paired off and are given the following instructions: Each person has a limit of where he will permit another to touch him. However this limit is not usually openly displayed. Your task is to find this limit in your partner and see if it can be stretched. Begin by deciding which person will touch and which will be passively touched. You decided who is to start. Begin, then, by touching your partner with your hands slowly and carefully. If the partner feels upset by a touch in a certain place, he will tell you. Continue until all limits are made clear. Now continue touching and see if these limits can be extended.

When one partner has finished, the roles are exchanged. It is important that the touching be gradual, and that the person being touched does not suffer, but makes it clear when a limit of touch is reached.

After both partners have explored and stretched the limits, they share their experiences with each other and with the whole group. It is important to see where and how resentments build up, and how satisfactions develop.

Deprivation of touch

After an experience of rich touching, group members are asked to isolate themselves as completely as possible from each other. If possible they are sent to separate rooms. If not they are covered with a sheet or bedspread and lights are extinguished. All sounds are turned off if possible. Individuals are asked to make themselves as relaxed as possible but not to sleep. Individuals are asked to breather deeply ten times and then go *into* themselves and experience themselves as fully as possible.

This is continued for at least ten minutes while movements are observed by one person not directly involved in the activity. The group is then reassembled, feelings and reactions are shared. If requested, the observer reports what he saw. On many occasions fear and sadness may develop in some subjects. If so, it should be allowed to flow and should be reported with everything else at the summing up of the activity.

Touch by water

This activity can usually only be done at home, but nevertheless is important enough to be assigned to each group member at an appropriate time.

Each person is asked to get into a shower of warm water (at least 95% Fahrenheit). He stands contemplating the stream of water and also his body. He focuses on each part of his body and touches it with his hands delicately. After 5 or 10 minutes of this, he turns the stream of water on himself and lets it move gradually over his body. He starts at whatever part interests him and moves the stream over his body as his fancy directs him. Eventually he covers each part of his body.

If some body parts seem dead or inert, the water is directed on them more strongly and then is moved about and the flow is varied in intensity. The stream is then moved to other parts and again back to the "dead" areas. This process continues for about half an hour.

After this, the body is gently dried and stretched out on a comfortable bed. If a large enough tub is available, the body is stretched in a tub of warm water before being dried.

While stretched in the tub or on the bed, a sensory survey is carried out to see what feelings are where. The whole experience is then shared with the group at the earliest opportunity.

Fantasies

The shrinking-expanding fantasy

Guided fantasies or day dreams have been described in chapter 11. These are very useful and many others are found in the references which follow this appendix. One fantasy which has proved useful to me involves having individuals radically change their size. The instructions for it are as follows:

Select a chair that interests you and that you would like to know better. Stand in front of it. Look at all the details of it. Touch it all over—top, back, seat, legs. Sit down by it and rub against it. Lie on the floor and look up under it. Do you feel you know it now? If not, do whatever else would further your knowledge of it.

Now, close your eyes and imagine yourself standing in front of your chair. Visualize it in all of its details. Then imagine yourself sitting in your chair. See what feelings you have!

Now gradually make yourself smaller. You are sitting in the chair but you are only three feet tall. Your legs do not hang over the seat at all! Now you are two feet tall! One foot! Six inches! Three inches! One inch! Stand on the seat of the chair and look at the immensity of it. How tall the arms! How very high the back! How very far down the floor as you peer over the edge of the seat!

Now make yourself even smaller. A half inch! A quarter inch! Imagine the legs of the chair are hollow and you have crawled inside one of them through a screw hole. You slide down one leg, the right front one, and survey what you find there. You crawl up the inside of the leg by a tiny ladder and walk across the chair frame (inside, of course) to the right rear leg. You explore it. You do similarly with all four legs and with the framework of the back of the chair. You stumble through the upholstery (if there is any). You finally come out and find yourself even smaller.

You are now microscopic in size. You can walk right into the wood of the chair through the scratches on the wooden frame. You are now walking between the cells of wood of which the chair is made. It is a mass of huge box-like structures. But you can crawl between these wood cells because you are so tiny. You explore all you see and all you can find in this jungle of cells.

Now you are out on the seat of the chair again and you have grown to one inch in size. You look around and decide to make yourself larger. You are two inches, three, four! Now you are a foot tall! Now two feet, three feet, four feet! Now you are your own size. You walk outside and keep on growing. You are seven feet tall now, eight feet, nine feet, ten feet! You move away from the buildings and trees so you will have room. You are still growing—fifteen feet, twenty feet, thirty feet! You look around you and survey the landscape. You are as tall as the buildings. You are as tall as the trees! You grow taller—forty feet, fifty feet, eighty feet, one hundred feet! There you stand *towering* over everything. What do you want to do? Whatever it is, you explore the scene as a giant, and you make yourself however large you want to be. (The growth here should be slow, taking ten to twelve minutes to accomplish.)

Now you have had your giant fling, so you start to come back. You are back to fifty feet in height. How you are thirty feet. You and the buildings are again the same. Twenty feet, ten feet, seven feet! And now you are your own size. You come back inside. You sit down. Your eyes are still closed, so you relax and think of all you have done. Now you gradually open your eyes.

Find yourself a partner and tell him what you experienced. After this all pairs will share their feelings, and touches, and sensations with the whole group. Changes in feelings from growing down to growing up will be important to note here. Also, which situations produce fear or anxiety? Which produce pleasure or joy?

Future fantasy

This exercise stretches the person ahead and often reveals many hidden personality traits. The directions are:

Close your eyes and breathe five deep breaths (see hand dialogue under Direct Touching). Now imagine you are five years older. It is five years from now—this very day, this very month! Where are you? What are you doing? Who is with you? Where do you live? How do you earn your living? What do you look like? How are you dressed? How do you wear your hair?

Stay with this situation and move with it and see where it carries you. This goes on for three or four minutes. Then pick a partner and tell him what you experienced. After this the sharing will move into the whole group and the whole experience will be interpreted to the extent that the participants desire. In this experience many new things may arise, particularly whether the future "appears" as enjoyable, whether it is fraught with problems, or whether it is just like the present!

Past fantasy

This exercise is a group-oriented experience. Participants are divided into groups of five. The instructions are as follows:

Look at each one of your group. Do not talk to them, just look at them quietly. Try to get the *feel* of what they are like. Now close your eyes. Reach out and touch the persons on each side of you. Take their hands and hold them for a minute. Now move your seat and move between the two persons you did not touch before. Hold their hands and get the *feel* of them, with your eyes closed.

Now separate yourself from your group. Turn your back toward them. Close your eyes and go into yourself. In your imagination, picture each of the other four of your group. See which one is clearest to you, and concentrate on this person.

Move back in time now and imagine this person ten years ago. What did he look like? What clothes is he wearing? How is his hair? What is he doing? Where does he live? Who are his companions? Stay with him for a few minutes and see what he does. Now gradually open your eyes and share you experiences with your group. Reactions of group members to others' perceptions of them ten years ago are important here. Feelings about the whole experience should be fully shared and interpreted.

Fantasy of irrational action

Chapter 14 deals with the value of irrational action. This activity gives the person a chance to practice irrational action without fear of punishment. The instructions are:

Close your eyes. Get your mind out of the problems and restrictions of today. Turn off your tensions and inhibitions and breathe deeply (see hand dialogue under Direct Touching.) Now assume you are suddenly freed of all sense of responsibility, but you are living in the same situation as you are now. Get in touch with your feelings. Is there something that you very much want to do but *can't* or *won't* because of what would happen? Go into your feelings about this. Perhaps there are several such acts. If so, select the one you *most* want to do. The one which would release you the most.

Now imagine this situation very clearly. Who does it involve? Where does it take place? Visualize the surroundings. Visualize the person involved. *Now do what you want to do!* That's right. Do it now! Forget the consequences. Follow it through in your imagination and see what takes place. How do they take it? How do you feel after you have done it? Okay, come back to reality and share your reactions with the whole group.

Some participants may be too inhibited to get very far with this activity and only tremble on the brink of *almost* doing it. Others may have a ball doing what they have always wanted to do. The discussion and sharing may heighten the experience and may encourage some to dive into the pool of irrationality and others to try it again.

After the discussion of the fantasy, the direction could move toward real life and the possibility of doing something irrational *really*. Here it would be desirable if each group member would decide what irrational act he would be *willing* to do during the next week. He might even be encouraged to role play doing this act. At the next group meeting the results of such irrational action might be discussed. (Needless to say, this activity would be highly destructive if presented to certain groups of adolescents or other persons who are already saturated with irrationality.)

Verbal Descriptions

Self-description minus put-downs

In this activity, each person is asked to describe himself as he sees himself in a few sentences. He is asked to make his description factual, to eliminate explanations and value judgements. Each person responds in his turn. Immediately following this, each person is asked to repeat his description and after each statement to add "and that's all right."

When each one has finished, feedback and comments are called for from the whole group. Feelings about doing this are important. So are changes in facial expression and voice quality in the two descriptions. Some will say, "But it *isn't* all right that I eat too much." Others may see that the appended words, "that's all right," mean only that I accept my action as part of me, and I accept me. If I really want to change this action, I can if I see me as a person who is worthwhile, valuable, and capable of change. In order to change, I must see me as a person worthy of change. A worthless person is not worth improving.

Description of mother (and reverse)

Each person is asked to describe and talk about his mother as she was when he last saw her. He is asked also to give his feelings about her.

After each one has done this, he is asked to picture his mother, shut his eyes for a minute and visualize her. He now opens his eyes and describes *himself* as his mother would do it, calling himself by name as she would do and giving her feelings about him.

This turns out to be a very touching and powerful activity usually. Often tears and emotions clog the throats of those who do this. Often the description *by* mother of son or daughter is more revealing of the son or daughter than the original description was.

Description of father (and reverse)

This activity is the same as the above except father is substituted for mother. It is often very moving but brings out different qualities from the previous exercise. It turns out to be more rewarding for daughters than sons, as a rule.

Verbal Dialogues

Expectations

In this activity participants are paired either with someone whom they are involved with who is *not* present, or with someone in the group with whom they seem to be involved. In either case each one, in his turn, is asked to list his expectations for his partner. For example, "I expect you to be on time! I expect you to answer me! I expect you to be honest!"

Next, each person is asked to respond with expectations which the absent partner might have for the subject. In so doing they speak for and take the part of the absent ones.

After the lists are presented, each "expecter" is asked to what extent he feels his partner *is capable of* living up to these expectations. He is next asked to what extent his partner *wants* to live up to these expectations. Finally he is asked what he wants to do with these expectations or what he wants his partner to do with them.

This is followed by a general discussion of expectations and what they mean as well as feedback on voices of subjects when the two lists were given and feelings which developed during the exercise. This activity fits well with chapter 15.

Responsibilities

This activity is similar to the previous one except that the topic is responsibility instead of expectations. Each participant addresses an absent person and says, "I take responsibility for . . ." and repeats this statement for as many things as he does and will take responsibility for.

He follows this with, "I will *not* take responsibility for . . ." and repeats this statement as many times as is necessary to cover all the items for which he will *not* take responsibility.

After each one has given his two lists, he responds for the absent person as the absent person would reply, giving two lists, one of responsibilities and one of nonresponsibilities. Each partner—present and absent—then comments in dialogue on the other's list, giving their feelings about it and reactions to it.

This is followed by a general feedback and discussion of voices, "touches," and feelings during the activity.

Resentments and appreciations

This is another paired activity. The participants here are attempting to release resentment toward someone else who is not present. Each one chooses some "resented" person who is not present and, in fantasy, presents him with his total load of resentments saying, "I resent this that you do! I resent the other that you do!" and so on until the resentments run out.

Then each participant responds for the absent resented one, giving his resentments of the participant.

This is followed by a list of appreciations given, first, by participant and then by absent one. Each statement is in the form, "I appreciate this which you do (or are)! I appreciate that which you do (or are)!"

At the end, there is a feedback on feelings, voices, etc., as in the other dialogues. This activity goes well with chapters 5, 6, 10.

Make the rounds

This activity fits in at many places in a group encounter where a participant is having difficulty relating to others or in stating clearly his feelings and opinions of himself. The confused one is asked to "make the rounds" of the group and encounter each person in a specific way.

Should the individual be a chronic self-put downer, he would be asked to tell each group member how worthless he is. If the individual feels alone and wants warmth, he is asked to make some demonstration of warmth to each person and contact them in some way. If the individual wants to carry out some plan in his life but says he can't, he is asked to tell each group member how or why he can't—or how he *will*! If the individual needs help and feels he can't get it, he is asked to make the rounds and ask for help.

In making the rounds, the individual gets to hear himself repeatedly and feel himself as he goes through the act. He becomes more *aware* during the act of making the rounds. This is reinforced in the feedback later on. By this procedure, he gains strength and greater inner control. He touches, a bit, his inner self.

Exchange of presents

This is an activity designed as the final conclusion of a series of group experiences or for bringing together the feelings of the group at the termination of some phase of their activities. The instructions are as follows:

Since we are ending this course (workshop, meeting, convention, etc.), it seems appropriate to exchange farewell presents with each other. You have not bought presents. But each of us, I am sure, has qualities which others would like to have. And each of us would also like to give what we have to another who wants it.

The leader then starts by selecting one person and asking for some quality of his, and in return offering him one of the leader's qualities. For instance, "Mary, I would like to have your smile and placid disposition, and in return I would like to give you my facility with words and ability to speak out." Or "Jim, I would like to have some of your strength and determination to succeed and in return I would like to give you some of my patience and understanding of people."

The process continues and the person who was chosen chooses another and does as the leader does in "exchanging gifts." Should a person choose someone who has already been chosen, he is asked to choose also another person who hasn't been chosen. When the final person is chosen, he gets to choose and distribute gifts to as many persons as he wants to exchange with. At the end, each one who wants to give and exchange other gifts has a chance to do so.

This activity usually produces a rosy glow of feeling, and most persons feel very touched by it. A feedback after this experience would be anticlimatic.

These activities are, of course, not all that could be presented. It is hoped that they may be of value to those who want a richer and deeper now experience. Those who want more, should consult the references in the reading list which follows.

Reading List

The following sources are selected to give added material in the field of humanistic psychology in general, and to supply a large wealth of touch- and feeling-oriented activities in particular. The list is brief, as it includes only the most recent sources which have been useful to me in designing methods for teaching and conducting encounter groups.

1. Assagioli, Roberto. *Psychosynthesis* (New York: Viking, 1965).
   This book is by the founder of psychosynthesis. It gives a valuable rationale and philosophy on which the search for an inner self is based. It is also rich in all kinds of awareness-producing activities.
2. Gunther, Bernard. *What to Do Till the Messiah Comes* (New York: Macmillan, 1971).
   This is the latest book by the author of *Sense Relaxation*. It is a beautiful photographic presentation of many touch and feeling activities and is done in creative poetry.
3. Keleman, Stanley. *Sexuality, Self, and Survival* (San Francisco: Lodestar Press, 1971).
   The author here presents his neo-Reichian ideas on the operation and structure of the body and how to keep it in working order. He also includes interesting dialogues on various applied problems of body operation as well as some perspectives for the future.

4. Lilly, John. *Programming and Metaprogramming in the Human Biocomputer* (Menlo Park, Calif.: Portola Institute, Whole Earth Catalog, 1970).
This is a unique approach to the human organism and how it operates. The author presents in detail his hypotheses and his beliefs about his findings. He also describes many techniques for exploring the sensory operation of the body. Particularly rich is his penetration into sensory deprivation and its consequences.

5. Lowen, Alexander. *The Betrayal of the Body* (London: Macmillan, 1969).
This book is by the founder of bioenergetics. He gives his theory of the body and how it operates as well as how body structure and personality are related. He includes interesting drawings of body structure by patients which illustrate their own disorders. He also gives many exercises for freeing the body of blocks to energy flow.

6. Perls, F. S. *Ego, Hunger and Aggression* (New York: Random House, 1969).
This is the most intelligible book on the theory and practice of gestalt therapy. The author, the founder of gestalt therapy, gives a very complicated but thorough theory of gestalt and follows it with a host of practical exercises. Particularly helpful are the exercises on concentration therapy.

7. Schutz, William C. *Here Comes Everybody* (New York: Harper & Row, 1971).
This is the latest book by the author of *Joy*. In it he gives a very sound rationale for the encounter group method. He explains and justifies "open" encounter and describes many techniques and activities for conducting this kind of activity. Particularly outstanding is the author's self-analysis and self-criticism in regard to the spiritual dimension.

8. *Psychology Today*, a most important periodical for participants and practitioners alike, is published by Communications Research Machines, Inc., Carmel Valley Road, Del Mar, Calif. 92014.
This periodical carries psychological articles of all kinds and regularly gives space to articles on body operation, feeling, and touch.

Index